MW00611475

101

Leadership Lessons From Baseball's Greatest Managers

Christopher Stolle

©2013 Coaches Choice. All rights reserved. Printed in the United States.

No part of this book may be reproduced, stored in a retrieval system, or transmitted, in any form or by any means, electronic, mechanical, photocopying, recording, or otherwise, without the prior permission of Coaches Choice. Throughout this book, the masculine shall be deemed to include the feminine and vice versa.

ISBN: 978-1-60679-249-0
Library of Congress Control Number: 2012955607
Cover design: Cheery Sugabo
Book layout: Studio J Art & Design
Front cover photo: US Presswirre

Coaches Choice
P.O. Box 1828
Monterey, CA 93942
www.coacheschoice.com

Dedication

For my father,
Thomas J. Stolle

Acknowledgments

First and foremost, I must thank Kristi Huelsing and Angie Perry at Coaches Choice for allowing me the opportunity to write this book. Thanks to Edward Hargrove for doing an excellent copyediting job. I also want to thank Jill R. Hughes for helping me revise my book proposal. Likewise, I wish to thank friends and colleagues for reviewing my manuscript: Tracey Goldenberg, Sarah Mottley, Brenna Echterling, Rachel Schilling, Beth McQueen, Athena Lane, Kendra Gard, Kedron Renfro, Laurie Sommers, and Christina Falcone.

I want to thank Mr. Randy Wisehart, my middle school language arts teacher, for allowing me to attend Opening Day in Cincinnati in 1990 if I wrote about my experience for class. I still have that story I wrote, and without his encouragement, I might never have pursued writing. And thank you to Mr. Lester, my fifth-grade teacher, who turned a lackluster student into someone with a passion for learning and a belief in his ability to communicate with words rather than fists.

Last but not least, I want to thank my dad for taking me to baseball games growing up. My dad was a sportswriter for more than 15 years, and I learned a lot about sports by watching games with him, including teamwork, commitment, and passion. His enthusiasm for his favorite teams rubbed off on me, and although I wish we had had many other kinds of conversations during our times together, I'm actually glad the last chat we had before he passed away was about sports. It's what brought us together, and I can't imagine anything better than sports to bond a father and his son.

Once upon a time, a human being attempted to hit an object with another object, and over time, that meaningless activity developed into a sport called baseball. Growing up in Indiana, I couldn't ignore basketball, but hearing Marty Brennaman and Joe Nuxhall on my radio—emanating from 700 WLW in Cincinnati—call Reds games during my youth in the late 1980s pulled me more and more toward becoming a feverish baseball fan. To this day, I readily admit that I prefer to play basketball, but if given a choice, I'd rather watch a baseball game. Thank you to all the men and women who have helped promote America's greatest pastime.

Contents

Preface

Baseball hasn't changed so much throughout the years that advice from 1869 can't be applied to situations and players in 2013—and beyond. Thus, I have included a great mix of Major League managers from many different eras, college coaches from different decades, and even a high school coach. Some might offer opposing viewpoints; some might agree on the most peculiar aspects; and some are just plain funny characters who have enlivened baseball and its many players, teams, and fans.

Indeed, you might find leadership lessons that seem to contrast with each other, but the general concept is to offer you—the baseball manager or coach or the workplace manager or supervisor—enough different options, opinions, and ideas to help you pick and choose those that suit your personality and your style as well as the environment in which you work. Life and baseball are all about perspective, but as you'll also find as you read this book, life and baseball are about fun.

I didn't find writing this book to be a labor of love. I didn't find it to be work at all. I looked at it as an opportunity to share some amazing men and human beings with you and to help you, your team, your players, your workers, your fans, your employers, and even your families reach goals and reach dreams. As many lessons in this book will show, life is incredibly short. Make the most of it in whatever way feels right to you—and ignore those who tell you you're doing it wrong.

Lesson #1: Expect Patience
Felipe Alou

*"Everyone should manage in the minor leagues
for a while. You learn the most important thing:
patience with the young players."*

Patience—along with racism and segregation—is something too many men in baseball have had to endure because of their skin color. No matter their talents and abilities, minorities have had no easy time gaining important positions with baseball teams—especially manager.

After Felipe Alou completed his 17-year all-star career spent mostly with the San Francisco Giants and the Milwaukee and Atlanta Braves, he became a Minor League manager in 1976 for the Montreal Expos farm system for 12 seasons—one of the few baseball-related opportunities then for minorities after their careers had ended. He won two championships in the minors, earning him a spot with the Major League team as a bench coach in 1992.

He thought it might take some time before he got a chance to become a full-fledged manager. But when the Expos started the 1992 season poorly, management elevated Alou to manager, making him the first Latino in Major League history to hold that position. Alou managed the team to 70 wins en route to a second-place finish. He then led the Expos to a 74-40 record in the strike-shortened 1994 season—the only year from 1991 to 2005 the Atlanta Braves didn't finish in first place—earning Alou the Manager of the Year award.

"I don't care about other people's expectations," Alou said. "I've always been a manager that has always had confidence. A lot. … I don't want to get into it all. But if I tell you all the names I was called over the course of a lifetime … I wouldn't be here now. I have expectations for me. Whatever people expect of me or think of me … I've put that behind me."

Patience helped Alou become the second Dominican player in modern baseball history (after Ozzie Virgil Sr.) and also helped him as a Minor League manager—and then as a Major League manager. But patience also means knowing what needs to be done in any given situation, and Alou had that ability.

"It's fun to play for an aggressive manager, and everybody knows how good he is. But there's more to it than just what's on the field. He respects us, gives us freedom, and until something needs to be said, he doesn't say much," said former Expos second baseman Mike Lansing.

"I'm not afraid to make mistakes," Alou said. "I've always felt if I'm going to go down, I'm going to go down on my own terms."

Leadership Lessons

On the Diamond: Take time each season to involve yourself in camps and in visiting with players who play in lower leagues than those you coach in. Doing so can help you to not only see what kind of talent might come through the system (and eventually to your team) but to also share with these players life lessons and baseball acumen that will keep players focused on becoming better players as well as better human beings. Young players, though, seldom have the talents that older players have developed, so remember to compliment strengths and run extra drills (and a variety of them) to enhance weaknesses. Being mindful about attention spans and recognizing that young athletes are often testing themselves in more than just baseball will allow coaches to exude a patient demeanor and help them focus on the details rather than the big picture.

In the Workplace: Bosses demand success *now*, coworkers need that information *now*, and customers require that product or this service *now*. Some people understand the dynamics involved in accomplishing a task; others have no interest in knowing. Not all your employees will work at the same pace, and deadlines aren't always the same for everyone. Thus, remember to take a deep breath before making requests. This will go a long way toward giving you the patience needed to ensure you're handling everyone in the best way possible.

Lesson #2: Stay Calm
Walter Alston

*"Look at misfortune the same way you look at success:
Don't panic. Do your best and forget the consequences."*

Alston spoke these words before the 1963 season after critics suggested that a more fiery manager might have helped the Los Angeles Dodgers win the pennant in 1962 after tying the San Francisco Giants with 102 wins but then losing two games in the three-game playoff series. His team clearly took this matter-of-fact philosophy to heart in 1963, as the Dodgers won the National League pennant by six games over the St. Louis Cardinals, and then proceeded to sweep the New York Yankees to win the World Series.

In Alston's 23 years at the helm for the Brooklyn and Los Angeles Dodgers, he guided the team to seven pennants and four World Series titles, including Brooklyn's only title (in 1955) before the team moved to Los Angeles in 1958. In fact, in just their second year in Los Angeles, the Dodgers won the World Series in six games over the Chicago White Sox.

Only three men—Joe McCarthy (7), Casey Stengel (7), and Connie Mack (5)—have won more World Series titles, and only four men—Stengel (10), John McGraw (10), McCarthy (9), and Mack (9)—have more pennants. But the road to success for Alston and the Dodgers was neither easy nor consistent.

Former Dodger pitcher Carl Erskine remembers a memorable moment from Alston's first season as Brooklyn manager in 1954: "We weren't playing too well, so Walt got us together and said: 'If you expect me to be a rah-rah manager, you're wrong. You're all good players. You know the price you have to pay. Now go out and do it.'" Although that team finished second to the crosstown rival New York Giants, it would cruise to a National League pennant and a World Series title over the Yankees in 1955.

Alston said this about his 1955 team and his general approach to managing: "To be a good manager you have to have good players. That's 100%, and I'm lucky. Very much so. This club is pretty much professionals who conduct themselves on and off the field as pros, and they don't get much discipline in that regard. I would like to treat everybody fair and square and equal with no pets or favoritism to anyone, and yet in order to get the best out of them, you may have to kick one in the pants or pat the other on the back, and if that's being fair, O.K. You try to treat everybody the same, but you've got to do it a little different way."

"Teaching students is very much like managing baseball players," he said. "You've got to encourage some, you've got to drive others, if you are going to get the best out of every individual."

Leadership Lessons

On the Diamond: Berating players for their errors will only compound their frustration. Save teaching moments for practice. In game situations, you need to remain diligent about keeping players concentrating on what's happening in the present—whether after a hit or after an error. You need to encourage your players to help a downtrodden player regain his focus and not become concerned about a bad swing or a ball he just couldn't field or accurately throw. It's time to prepare for the next batter or the next opportunity. Success will come more easily—and rewards seem much more sweeter—when players can have fun playing baseball and not see every game as a life-or-death situation.

In the Workplace: If you find your employees making more mistakes than usual or feeling indifferent about their responsibilities, you should have them reassess their approach to work. Routines are effective in helping with motivation, but they can quickly become boring and limiting if workers don't switch up tasks now and again or fulfill aspects of their job in a different order than usual. What if they did their job backward? Have them try doing at 10 a.m. a task they usually take on at 4 p.m. to see if that makes any difference in how productive they are throughout that day. Don't panic if you don't see immediate results. Give them some time to determine if their new approaches are helping or hindering, and continue to encourage your workers to adjust their routines as needed.

Lesson #3: Dedicate Your Focus
Sparky Anderson

"Baseball is a simple game. If you have good players,
and if you keep them in the right frame of mind,
then the manager is a success. The players make
the manager; it's never the other way."

When the Cincinnati Reds hired George "Sparky" Anderson in 1970 to manage the team, the headline in the *Cincinnati Enquirer* read: "Sparky Who?" It didn't take Reds fans long to figure out, especially after Anderson immediately led the team to a 102-60 record, winning the National League West by 14.5 games, and sweeping the Pittsburgh Pirates in the NLCS for the National League pennant, although the Reds would lose the World Series to the Baltimore Orioles in five games.

"I remember that day in spring training when he told me 'I'm here to win and I want you to help me,'" Hall of Famer and former Reds first baseman Tony Perez said. "Right then, he had everybody. He wasn't saying, 'Listen to me, I'll get you there.' He was saying "Help me get us there.'"

Eventually, fortune would shine on the Reds, as the Big Red Machine won the 1975 and 1976 World Series titles—the last time a National League team has won consecutive championships. At his Hall of Fame induction in 2000, Anderson explained his role with the Reds and later with the Detroit Tigers, where he won another World Series. "Let me tell you this, and get it straight, and I hope every manager that follows me will listen very carefully: players earn this, by their skills," he said. "Managers come here, as I did, on their backs, for what they did for me. I never believed different, I will never believe different, and I think that's what made my career so lucky."

Anderson's teams always had something special about them: a commitment to winning borne from their manager's desire for each player to contribute his best.

"I have seen many players with potential who didn't go anywhere. They didn't want it badly enough. They didn't want to sacrifice. It comes down to one word—dedication," Anderson said. "If you've got a group that wants to win, you've got to let them."

As the first manager to win a World Series in both leagues (matched later by Tony La Russa), Anderson felt fortunate to have had the chance to manage in baseball.

"There's two kinds of managers," he said. "One that ain't very smart. He gets bad players, loses games, and gets fired. Then there was somebody like me that was a genius. I got good players, stayed out of the way, let 'em win a lot, and then just hung around for 26 years. It was a lot of fun."

Leadership Lessons

On the Diamond: What's the right frame of mind for your players? What do the players want to accomplish? What are their goals? While coaches need to have goals for their players, those players need to decide their own personal goals rather than have them continually thrust upon them. Good players know their limits, but they also know when it's time to push themselves a little harder. Try to encourage your players as often as possible to not just reach their goals, but to extend past them—even if just a little. But, if you constantly push players past their known limits, then players are apt to become burnt out or they might fail intentionally, forcing coaches to bench them for poor play. Baseball is indeed a simple game, and coaches shouldn't have to remind players to have fun. That should be an everyday, unspoken mantra. Allow your team to come together on its own. In this way, players will recognize their potential, they'll work toward achieving what they can, and they'll willingly make the manager—that's *you*—look good through their efforts.

In the Workplace: It doesn't take much to help your workers focus on their tasks at hand if they have clearly defined responsibilities and goals. Whiteboards—even electronic ones—that offer succinct methods to accomplish tasks will give workers something to consult for motivation and for them to ensure they're doing what's needed. Keep the advice simple but effective. That is, your suggestions should offer actions, not merely motivational words.

Lesson #4: Position Yourself for Success

Cap Anson

"Round up the strongest men who can hit a baseball the farthest the most often, put yourself on first base, and win."

Although Adrian "Cap" Anson didn't create the player-manager position, he had more success in this role than any player before or since because he played almost his entire career as player-manager. In his first seven full seasons as player-manager for the Chicago White Stockings (now the Cubs) from 1880 to 1886, his team won the National League pennant five times, including his first three years. In 1897, at age 45, he became the first batter to collect 3,000 hits—a feat no one else would achieve until Honus Wagner and Nap Lajoie did so in 1914. In fact, Wagner was a rookie in Anson's last season, with Lajoie starting his career in 1896.

In Anson's day, hitting a home run involved either hitting the ball beyond the outfielders (who had no wall behind them) or over a fence (if a field had a fence; if it did, it wasn't that far away), but players tended to prefer to, as "Wee Willie" Keeler said, "Keep your eye clear, and hit 'em where they ain't," meaning players tried to hit line drives between fielders. Hits—singles, bunts, and the like—were more common than home runs. Thus, if a player could single through the infield to get to first base, the team would find a way to bring him in via similar techniques.

No player hit better than Anson during the White Stockings' pennant years, and until the American League formed in 1901, no team/manager combination in any other professional league—save for Frank Selee and his 1890–1901 Boston Beaneaters (now the Atlanta Braves)—achieved more team goals than Chicago.

"The secret of the club's success in those days lay in its team work, and in the fact that a goodly portion of the time was spent in studying and developing the fine points of the game, which long practice made them fairly perfect in. There were one or two weak spots in its make-up, but so well did it perform as a whole that these weak spots were quite apt to be lost sight of when the time for summing up the result of the season's play had arrived," Anson wrote in *A Ball Player's Career*, his 1900 autobiography.

Leadership Lessons

On the Diamond: A hit is a hit is a hit, and if it scores runs, then it doesn't matter how it happens. While fans love to see home runs, and players love to him them, you can expose a team's defensive weaknesses as well as stun your opponents through playing small ball: bunts, hit-and-run plays, stealing, sacrifice flies, and strong pitching. If a situation seems ripe for such a play, why not take advantage of a possible mismatch and attempt to disrupt a team through one of these tactics? While it seems wasteful to lose an out just to score a run, doing this is easier in a close game rather than a game where one team has a large lead, although history has many examples of teams coming back in such games by playing small ball. If your team has the right assets, it can benefit from getting back to fundamentals and not trying to hit home runs every at bat.

In the Workplace: Trying to accomplish too much at once can prove detrimental to you and your staff as well as your collective and individual goals. Breaking tasks into smaller steps will help your staff build confidence because each person can check off a step and move on to the next one and not feel like he has to knock out a huge chunk. Likewise, if everyone touches every project he has at least once a day, then every project will move forward—taking into consideration, of course, priorities and deadlines.

Lesson #5: Persist Against Resistance
Dusty Baker

"When you fail, get up and try it again. Failure is when you cease to dream, when you cease to try to get better."

Johnnie B. "Dusty" Baker has made a name for himself as a no-nonsense manager who makes decisions based on his gut rather than the numbers or even pressure from outside forces. And he has had success with this, leading the San Francisco Giants, the Chicago Cubs, and the Cincinnati Reds to five playoff appearances in his 19 seasons.

Baker knows it's vital to "not be afraid to be different and separate yourself from the pack. And that goes for the time that you're willing to put in. … Go against what the masses say to do," he said. But Baker also knows that having a passion and pursuing it can make taking that lone path all the more sweeter when you reach the journey's end.

"Dedication, desire, and love for what you're doing [are important qualities]. Because once you fall in love with what you're doing, then you explore other avenues and see things you might not have seen before," he said. "I think you have to spend countless hours pursuing that, practicing, reading, doing whatever you can to learn more about what you're doing and more about yourself."

Leadership Lessons

On the Diamond: You often achieve your dreams as a coach vicariously through your players. Thus, take time to write down specific goals for you as a coach and as a human being that depend on you and your actions. Maybe you desire to yell less and lead by example more. Maybe you want to improve how you handle tough situations and how you allow your team to celebrate wins. Perhaps you want to ensure you spend more time with your family. When you write down your goals and dreams and share them with someone—to help maintain accountability—then you have a better chance at reaching them.

In the Workplace: You might have requirements from your supervisor—because even a manager has a boss—to submit yearly goals and expectations. But you should also have a list for yourself that expresses goals and dreams you have that don't depend on what your employees achieve with you as their manager. You should let someone else read this list to be an advocate for you, but make sure your goals and dreams depend on your actions and what you can do to improve in your capacity. You might have expectations that don't quite sum up your desires; this list is that chance to do that. And remember to reward yourself when you reach a goal.

Lesson #6: Determine Your Requirements

Greg Beals

*"The difference between the good and the great baseball
players are the guys that learn how to deal with the game
and the ins and outs and ups and downs."*

After eight years at Ball State University, where he won 243 games and three Mid-American Conference division championships, Greg Beals now coaches baseball at Ohio State University.

Coach Beals looks for three important aspects for potential recruits to have:
- *Good grades:* These give a coach one less thing to worry about.
- *Energy and enthusiasm:* Showing a passion for the game means a player will make a commitment toward team and individual goals.
- *Competitiveness:* How a player reacts in certain hitting, running, and fielding situations can give a coach great insight into his demeanor.

But Coach Beals knows that once players are on campus and have adjusted to new surroundings, he needs to have ways to offer feedback to them. His new philosophy revolves around ensuring players are having quality at bats.

"I'm trying to motivate the way our players focus on the things that they can control and things that they can grasp a hold of. Normally players get motivated from the scoreboard or get motivated from their batting average, but I want to motivate and talk to them about things that are a little deeper than that," he said. "We keep track of quality at bats and hard hit average and have a point system that's based off of getting on base, moving runners, and driving runners in. That way the players have something to learn from even if they don't get a hit because this is a game of failure and we as coaches need to find different ways of giving them feedback that is process driven and not just result driven."

Leadership Lessons

On the Diamond: What do you look for when you watch players at a tryout? What characteristics are important for you and your team and your program? Your players reflect your vision, and fans notice coaches who can't control disruptive players—and often have plenty to say about them. How do you want to represent yourself?

In the Workplace: If you have a chance to hire new employees for your team, what are some critical traits you look for from them? Aside from their abilities to do the work, what kind of people do you want them to be? You can't find that out from a resume, so make sure you ask pointed questions in interviews—being careful not to ask anything too personal—and ensure this person will fit in with the dynamic you're trying to create in your work environment.

Lesson #7: Rearrange Your Arrangements
Bob Bennett

*"Strategy is rarely so simple as using a
prescribed solution to every situation."*

Bob Bennett coached at Fresno State for 34 years, won more than 1,300 games, and ended his career with 26 straight winning seasons—and just two losing seasons. He led the Bulldogs to more than 20 NCAA tournaments and two College World Series appearances, notching 17 conference titles, 32 All-Americans, and nine first-round draft picks.

In *The Baseball Coaching Bible*, Coach Bennett discussed how to put together a batting order:

- *Leadoff hitter:* "The leadoff hitter should be emotional and aggressive, yet patient." A player who knows right away what he needs to do will fill this role quite well.
- *Second hitter:* "Place a premium on this hitter's ability to make contact and bunt." If the first batter has speed, this hitter needs to know what he can do to help move him forward—whether via a bunt or gaining a good count to help him steal a base.
- *Third hitter:* "The hitter in the number 3 spot is generally the best overall hitter in the lineup. Consistency is extremely important." This batter will often have more at bats than those who follow him, so ensuring this player has speed and power will increase his ability to have quality plate appearances.
- *Fourth hitter:* "The most important attribute to consider in selecting the batter for the cleanup spot is his ability to hit in pressure situations, with men in scoring position." Many teams have power hitters in this spot, but if one or two of the first three hitters make it to base, then even a single can gain a run.
- *Fifth hitter:* "This hitter should be similar to the fourth hitter. If two hitters on your club have similar attributes, place the more consistent one in the fourth spot. Put the one with the most power in the fifth spot." Many teams haven't subscribed to this theory, but during the course of a game, this hitter could have a chance to drive in many runs.
- *Sixth hitter:* "Choose either a batter similar to the leadoff hitter or a batter with power." Compare this player with others before him, and also keep in mind your own strategies for scoring runs. This player can benefit the team in close games by being good at bunting or using other means to reach base. But he can also be a power hitter who can clean up the bases if a situation requires it. Someone with a good mix of these abilities will work best for any tactic you might wish to employ.
- *Other hitters:* "The players who bat in the seventh through nine spots may be outstanding defensive players with limited hitting skills." For most teams, these positions include an infield position, the catcher, and the pitcher—in that order. For these and previous batters, consider alternating left-handed hitters and

right-handed hitters as often as your team's makeup will allow. Sometimes, you might have a weaker hitting lineup but a strong defensive team on the field, depending on your opponent and how you need to play certain hitters.

Leadership Lessons

On the Diamond: What works today might not work tomorrow. Putting together a lineup is sometimes a guess, but once you see what works with any given batting order, you can make adjustments as necessary. But don't stick with the status quo; that is, maybe you want a weaker hitter to take his turns early or you want to bump up a catcher (Johnny Bench batted cleanup; Yogi Berra batted fifth; and Jason Kendall batted leadoff many times in their careers)—and don't let someone's struggles force you to move him to another spot in the lineup or drop him from it completely. That said, don't take last night's hero from today's lineup just because the pitching matchup isn't favorable. You're giving him the sense that his performance was an anomaly. Why not play him and let him take advantage of his confidence?

In the Workplace: What works for some might not work for all. Sometimes, you have to allow workers to accomplish tasks in whatever way works for them—as long as they're not preventing someone else from doing the same. Businesses tend to try to thrive on processes and consistent strategies. But a one-size-fits-all mentality often backfires because it constrains employees and essentially forces them to become robots who take on every task the same way.

Lesson #8: Share Sage Advice
Yogi Berra

"You're never out of it till you're out of it."

Perhaps no player or manager has had more books written about what he said—or might have said or outright didn't say—than Yogi Berra, who managed the New York Yankees to an American League pennant in 1964 and the New York Mets to a National League pennant in 1973. His childhood friend, former Major League catcher Joe Garagiola, said: "If he tells you something, he may not be able to explain it as well as somebody else, but you can go to the bank on it."

People in business and management as well as in many different sports—not just baseball—have incorporated Yogisms into their everyday activities:

- *"If you don't know where you're going, you might not get there."* If you have a plan, you might just end up to where you *do* want and need to go. Plans can help you make changes when you realize you're starting to head to somewhere you *don't* want or need to go.

- *"Never answer an anonymous letter."* If people aren't willing to stand up for their convictions and be honest with their thoughts and feelings, why respond to veiled comments? People need only answer to those who will confront them, challenge them—and support them.

- *"I usually take a two-hour nap from one to four."* This isn't about a three-hour nap. It's about planning when to fit in a nap—or a break or a different activity—during a busy day when some rest will certainly help reenergize you.

- *"When you come to a fork in the road, take it."* Although Yogi said this about how to get to his house (he lived on a circular road), this idea really means being able to make a decision and stick with it. It echoes Robert Frost's "Yet knowing how way leads on to way/I doubted if I should ever come back" but also counters Led Zeppelin's "Yes, there are two paths you can go by, but in the long run/There's still time to change the road you're on."

- *"You can observe a lot by watching."* Replace "observe" with "learn" or "understand," and the meaning becomes a little clearer. But just as people can listen and yet not hear, they can also watch but not see. Ultimately, this means paying attention to surroundings and determining what's best to do to meet needs.

- *"The future ain't what it used to be."* And the future certainly isn't what people in decades past imagined it might be. Everyone is part of what the future is or isn't. Life changes, and people should try to acclimate themselves to change but also become part of transformations as well as suggest ways to improve what's being done now.

- *"It ain't over till it's over."* Keep playing until everything has been settled. Baseball has never had a clock to determine what happens when. If players keep fighting until the end, anything is possible. Teams can decide how to react to losing situations, but when individual attitudes undermine that team emotion, it can prove detrimental to a game or to an entire season.

Leadership Lessons

On the Diamond: More than just baseball managers have offered great quotes. Why not type up some of your favorite sports quotes; lines from books, music, and movies; and even advice you find in fortune cookies, and then offer them before each game and each practice to help your team focus on a specific concept for that day.

In the Workplace: Each day, offer via email or a bulletin board a quote from a successful businessperson or political leader or even a comedian, and express your thoughts on how these words can help your employees during that day's work. Keep it simple, but ensure what you offer is relevant, not just words that might make someone laugh or raise an eyebrow.

Lesson #9: Extend Your Efforts
Skip Bertman

*"No one can truly be successful by doing only
what is required of them. Reaching a little higher
is the amount of effort over and above the
required that determines true excellence."*

Perhaps no team in college baseball had more success from 1990 to 2000 than Skip Bertman's LSU Tigers. They won six Southeastern Conference championships and five College World Series, and they led the nation in collegiate baseball attendance from 1996 to 2001.

Coach Bertman established an attitude—a team covenant—that everyone on his teams had to agree to adhere to and then sign a written agreement to attest to that promise. Along with the team motto, his covenant also included these requirements:

- *Creating synergy:* Coach Bertman believed in playing his best nine, not his nine best. Sometimes, certain players will play better together than others. Likewise, two people's collective efforts might equal more than their individual efforts combined.

- *Taking one step at a time:* Many pieces make up a whole in baseball—from players to uniforms to practice elements and even such aspects as to how comfortable fans are in the stands. Each part might seem small and insignificant, but each can help a team build from total chaos to effortless symbiosis.

- *Believing in miracles:* Just because something has happened before doesn't mean it will happen again. Likewise, just because something hasn't happened doesn't mean it can't. Coaches can make little changes to help position their teams for success. And it has to do with what Coach Bertman calls LUCK: Laboring Under Correct Knowledge.

- *Taking responsibility:* Players can hurt a team through their own blame game. They must take responsibility for how they carry themselves as well as how they go about admitting their mistakes—and then learning from them.

- *Playing for excellence:* Coach Bertman knows players can choose between two doors: one marked "Win," and one marked "Fail." But he offered them a third choice: "Excellence." Choosing that door means players represent themselves, their school, their faith, their families, and even their coaches through their best efforts.

"Players on my team know they are welcome anytime through door number three, win or lose. Actually, winning can't be the most important thing when several hundred baseball teams suit up every year and only one can win the national championship," said Coach Bertman. "Trying to win and being the best you can be, both on and off the field—those are the important things."

Leadership Lessons

On the Diamond: You can't win a game in one inning, but you can make a difference in the first inning that will help you not have to work so hard in the late innings. When you encourage your team to give its best effort right away and to reach a little higher in the early innings, then the workload might lessen by game's end. While players might know what they need to do, encourage them to strive for something beyond that when they can.

In the Workplace: Some projects might seem to go on endlessly. You can help your employees build confidence in two diverse ways: Start with the hard work to make easier tasks even easier or start with small jobs to build motivation to tackle harder responsibilities. Try to allow your employees to do what works best for them, but always encourage them to keep striving for something better and to put in the needed effort for that.

Lesson #10: Showcase Your Attitude
Bruce Bochy

"The biggest thing is to have a swagger when you take the field. When you're not going well, you have to change something—the biggest thing is the way you carry yourself. You have to walk like you belong with the best, go up to the plate like you know you belong with the best. That's swagger."

Indeed, swagger would certainly have been a needed ingredient for the 2010 Giants to win the franchise's first World Series since 1954 and its first since moving to the Bay Area (and for the team to win another World Series in 2012).

Bruce Bochy has quietly had a successful managerial career with the San Diego Padres and the San Francisco Giants. Tim Milburn, who works with young leaders and loves sharing leadership resources, summed up Bochy's five best leadership ideas:

- *Keep your team focused:* "You certainly can't drift mentally … when you're not putting a lot of runs on the board and playing these tight games," Bochy said. Baseball seasons are rife with distractions, and Bochy isn't afraid to make personnel changes *during* a season to help eliminate them.

- *Do what's best for the team:* "You set aside your own agenda and do what's best for the team. That's what it has to be at this point. Hopefully we have one priority, and that's to win. These guys have done a great job with it," Bochy said. "A lot of guys who have been out there every day, their role has changed. They've done a great job of being a good teammate and accepting that and doing whatever they can to help out. It's not easy. They all want to be a part of it but there are only nine places out there."

- *Know what people are good at:* "I don't know if I'm managing really any different than what I was doing earlier. It's not so much ruffling feathers, it's doing what's right and putting the guys out there that you think are going to help you win that game," Bochy said.

- *Put your people in a position to succeed:* "When you put together a club, hopefully you have guys who are unified," Bochy said. "You have that chemistry. And that's not something that just happens. You have to work at it. These guys do."

- *Build unity through a common purpose:* "Unity doesn't come from everyone agreeing on everything. Unity comes from pursuing a common purpose. Sometimes you take the scenic route to get there and there's lots of discussion, arguments, and pushback. But you arrive … together. Chemistry is formed through the mutual respect each member of the team has for the other. Once again, people may not see things eye to eye, but they don't dismiss someone simply because the other person holds a different viewpoint," Milburn said. "When a leader communicates a clear and compelling vision for the team and the members buy into it, unity and chemistry can flourish. When there's confusion and many false starts because a team doesn't know where it's going, chemistry disintegrates and unity is only superficial at best."

Leadership Lessons

On the Diamond: Winning a championship is every team's goal, but because only one team can do that each season, try to focus on building team chemistry and unity through achieving smaller goals. Essentially, you want your team to improve from its last game, and if the team falters or isn't consistent, this is a time to discuss swagger: what you can do as a coach and what they can do as players to *show* they're good at what they do.

In the Workplace: If times are hectic in your office and deadlines come fast and furious, set small yet realistic and achievable goals every day. Help your employees have a reason to carry their heads high even in trying times. This also helps to build unity because they're achieving a goal and helping the team move forward by completing their parts of the whole.

Lesson #11: Strive for Awareness
Lou Boudreau

"This is reaching the top. That's what we all strive for no matter what profession we're in."

Lou Boudreau spoke these words after being voted into baseball's Hall of Fame in 1970. When the 24-year-old shortstop became the Cleveland Indians' manager in 1942, he became the youngest manager in baseball history—a record that still remains—and would have to prove he could take the team to its own pinnacle: a World Series title.

Although Boudreau joined the team in 1938, he had been the Indians' everyday shortstop in 1940 and 1941 and felt ready to take over after the team fired manager Roger Peckinpaugh. Owner Bill Veeck—with support from many of the players—agreed, and Boudreau would manage the team through the 1950 season. He would later manage the Boston Red Sox, the Kansas City Athletics, and the Chicago Cubs, but he made his mark—as a player and as a manager—in Cleveland.

In 1948, the Indians—and the "Boy Manager" especially—would achieve quite an accomplishment by winning the World Series against the Boston Braves. For Boudreau, the victory became even sweeter when he won the American League MVP that season—beating out Joe DiMaggio and Ted Williams by an almost unanimous vote. No player-manager had achieved this dual feat before and none have done so since.

Oddly enough, it was Boudreau who threw out DiMaggio during his final at bat on July 17, 1941, ending Joltin' Joe's 56-game hitting streak. Boudreau also created the Williams shift, forcing the left-handed Splendid Splinter to try to hit to left field rather than into a defensively loaded right side.

"It would be awfully hard to do both jobs today, but back then it worked out all right. When a player/manager is a shortstop, as I was most of the time, you're deeply involved in the game anyway. Your head's right in the action, where a manager should be," Boudreau said.

"In the World Series, he directed his outfielders, had to think of his bullpen, and I often wondered whether he was giving signs to his catcher," former manager and Hall of Fame infielder Frankie Frisch said about Boudreau. "When I think of Boudreau, I must say he was one of the great shortstops and also a great leader—an inspiration to a club and a fellow to set an example."

Leadership Lessons

On the Diamond: If you're not a manager who goes out in the field while your team plays a simulation game, grab your glove and head to the field. Take time to see what your players see by switching to a different position each inning. You might even learn something about yourself while you're out there, but take mental notes about observations you make about your players.

In the Workplace: Spend some time for a few weeks as a job shadow for each employee you supervise. What do you notice about them or about the work involved that you didn't know before. Perhaps you'll also discover some new ways to go about managing your employees, and you should assuredly learn something about yourself.

Lesson #12: Enjoy the Adventures
Bobo Brayton

"The journey on the way to winning is the fun of baseball."

Chuck "Bobo" Brayton coached Washington State University from 1962 to 1994, and his 1,162 wins are still a school record. His Cougars won 21 conference titles in the Pac-8/Pac-10, and he took teams to the College World Series in 1965 and 1976. Coach Brayton helped develop 23 Major League players, including pitcher Aaron Sele and first baseman John Olerud, who was the National Player of the Year in 1988.

"Bobo made you grow up fast, but in a very caring environment," Sele said. "He demanded a lot of you on the field, and he demanded a lot of you as a student-athlete. … Bobo really helped me grow up."

"It definitely took me a while getting comfortable around Bobo," Olerud said. "The more you got to playing with him and got to know him and his personality, his great sense of humor and his heart, you just couldn't help but love the guy. He was just such a big influence for me."

Coach Brayton expanded on his "fun" philosophy in *The Baseball Coaching Bible* by detailing suggestions on how to add fun to your program:

- *Team meetings:* "By adding a little fun to team meetings you will build camaraderie, fellowship, and leadership. Cocoa and cookies is a good beginning."
- *Locker room:* "The locker room might include a sign pertinent to the moment, the orders of the day, a place to rest, some good music, occasional joking, and light horseplay."
- *On the field:* Have fun with lingo, conversations among players, and playing games with drills. Remind players that fans are coming to see them play and want to be entertained. Good practices will lead to enjoyable games.
- *Dugout and bullpen:* Keep players busy if they're not playing today—charting pitchers or warming up pitchers or keeping stats—and make sure they remember to have fun while keeping the dugout and bullpen tidy, as if it's all some kind of game.
- *Off the field:* "Know your players—the good things and the amusing things, what they do, who they run around with, their problems, their strengths and weaknesses, their parents, where they come from. Give your players support and help."
- *Giving back:* Hold autograph sessions or have the players give clinics to young players or visit hospitals to share their personal stories with sick and injured people.

Leadership Lessons

On the Diamond: Philosopher Ralph Waldo Emerson said, "Life is a journey, not a destination." What are you doing during this journey to help your players enjoy themselves while also learning about life? You can learn more about yourself after a loss than a win, and losing isn't the usual destination. But losing is a process by which you recalculate your internal GPS and recognize where you truly need and want to go. How can you make that fun for your players?

In the Workplace: Some workplaces seem stiff with regimented processes and nose-to-the-grindstone attitudes. How can you help your employees change things up and infuse some fun into their daily routines? How can you keep everyone's focus on work, yet make the atmosphere a little more relaxing and less stressful? It doesn't have to be like Willy Wonka's chocolate factory, but it doesn't have to be purgatory either.

Lesson #13: Reconsider Your Goals
Jim Brock

*"It just doesn't matter what people think you are or what
you can be. Who cares, anyway? It comes down to how
well you think you can do and how well you do, and
are your goals important enough for you to reach them."*

Just three days after his Arizona State University baseball team lost in the College World Series in 1994, Jim Brock lost his battle with cancer. In his short 23 years with the Sun Devils, he won more than 1,000 games, won the College World Series in 1977 and 1981, and earned the National Coach of the Year award four times.

"There has to be a certain amount of pride that goes into what you do. Someday, you'll all be as old as I am now, and I don't want you to look back and think you didn't make the most out of this. This all goes by very, very fast. Make the ... most of it," Coach Brock said to his players before that College World Series in 1994.

Coach Brock would never say "It's just a game" because he knew he had an opportunity to make a difference in young men's lives.

"A coach is an actor. You might want to be angry, but it might not be when they need anger. Or the other way around," he said. "If you lose your cool for a second, then your anger serves as a slap in the face for them. That's fine. But you can't ever lose sight of the fact that you're an actor and the ball club is your audience. You have to play them just right."

In a May 1994 article in the *Phoenix New Times*, writer Paul Rubin summarized Coach Brock and his paradoxes that most coaches likely deal with on a daily basis:

He is a born-again Christian who nonetheless rails against "'God's plan' types who tell other people how to think. ..."

He's spent his life surrounded by jocks, but it's never troubled him that his only son's best weapon is his mind.

He's obsessed with winning, but maintains such a hard line on discipline that he has suspended front-line players at the College World Series for breaking team rules he could have ignored.

He is a supremely confident coach who wonders yet if his boss and the public appreciate his accomplishments.

Leadership Lessons

On the Diamond: Everyone is dealing with situations away from the field, and those circumstances should help define who you are and how you handle those issues, not be what constricts you. Being a baseball coach is but one aspect of who you are. Don't let that determine your entire existence. But at the same time, what can you do in that role to ensure baseball isn't all that players have going for them?

In the Workplace: When the day ends and everyone goes home, do you continue to think about work and what you need to accomplish or what your team needs to do? Take time to deal with other situations in your life. Do something fun. Pursue a new hobby. Let life take you in some new directions before your time on this planet has ended. Make a difference in your own life—and that will help you make a difference in others' lives.

Lesson #14: Demand Courage
Bill Carrigan

*"The first great requisite for success in baseball is nerve.
I have seen players with speed, hitting, strength,
and grace, but they did not make good. They lack
the prime essential, stoutness of heart."*

Despite his short managerial career, Bill Carrigan left a significant mark on the Boston Red Sox franchise, including winning two World Series titles in 1915 and 1916. He initially ended his playing and managing career after the 1916 World Series to spend more time with his family in his native Maine (returning to manage the team from 1927 to 1929), but he helped set a standard for future player-managers.

Carrigan managed his teams like he played: tough, fearless, and demanding—earning him his "Rough" nickname. Because he played catcher, he understood how to call a game, he wasn't afraid to block even the great Ty Cobb from touching home plate, and he didn't allow Tris Speaker, his own teammate and charge, to intimidate him. In fact, Babe Ruth, then a pitcher and also Carrigan's one-time roommate, acknowledged how much his manager helped him develop on and off the field by calling him the best manager he ever had.

Before the 1914 season, after a fourth-place finish in 1913, Carrigan—now helming the club full time after Jake Stahl had been relieved of his duties after 80 games in 1913—didn't make a prediction about his team's fate as much as he tried to send his players a message: "I am leading a team of game determined fighters, men who will go after every game as though the championship depended on it. We will be heard from all through the season." Although the 1914 team would finish in second place, 8.5 games behind the Philadelphia Athletics, Carrigan had set a revitalized tone for a franchise that had won the World Series in 1912.

One way Carrigan helped strengthen relationships on his team was by organizing such group activities as fishing, golfing, and riding during spring training, and the team had an extra incentive to perform well in 1915 because the National League's Boston Braves had swept the heavily favored and 1913 American League champion Philadelphia Athletics in 1914. But a resurging and young Red Sox team didn't have to worry about an A's team that lost stars Eddie Collins and Nap Lajoie, thus ensuring the A's would finish in last place in not only 1915 but also 1916. Detroit and Chicago provided just enough competition to make the Red Sox earn their pennants, but in the World Series, Boston beat the Philadelphia Phillies in 1915 and the Brooklyn Robins in 1916 by losing just one game each series.

Until 2004 and 2007 came around, those early Red Sox teams might have remained the best collection of talent Boston had ever put on a field at one time—and Carrigan might still remain as the Red Sox's all-time best manager. Without question, though, Carrigan provided that team with the heart it needed to know how to compete in any given situation, especially dire ones.

Leadership Lessons

On the Diamond: Talent can take players only so far. Many players throughout the history of professional baseball have come and gone because they couldn't live up to their potential. More often than not, this was because they lacked dedication to the craft of hitting or fielding or pitching. Players need to put their heart—their passion, their drive, their dreams—into their efforts. And not merely for individual success, but to help the team reach its collective goal: winning games. Coaches can help players develop and strengthen their heart by putting aloof players through drills that require them to test themselves in skills not related to baseball, such as kicking soccer balls, throwing footballs, and swimming laps. While some players might discover hidden talents or other passions—and good for those who do—most will find that baseball suits them best, thereby boosting their confidence and increasing their heart. But don't let some players become Grinches toward other players or spoil the baseball experience for those who have a passion for the game.

In the Workplace: Business climates don't often lend themselves to workers showcasing their passions on a daily basis, but in small ways, you can show your dedication to your tasks. One way is to anticipate assignments and start putting together outlines and plans for tackling those projects when they're assigned to you. And if they're not assigned to you, you can share those ideas with those who are, thus lessening the demands on them. Likewise, although people would love for employers to offer extra training and perhaps even fun retreats to attend, nothing can keep you from venturing out on your own or in small groups to gain more knowledge, to grow together as a team, and to enhance yourselves professionally and personally. You know your talents, and you can't always depend on others to help bring them out. You must find those ways on your own—and then blow people away with your attitudes and your actions.

Lesson #15: Eliminate Errors

Pat Casey

"The line between winning and losing is so fine that it comes down to some of the simplest mistakes you can make."

Oregon State baseball coach Pat Casey knows a thing or two about winning. His Beavers won the 2006 College World Series and then repeated in 2007 despite a losing record in the Pac-10 Conference and being unranked nationally.

Coach Casey also knows something about leadership and its trials. "Leadership is a very difficult thing because it's easy to be a leader when things are going well. It's very difficult to be a leader when things are not going well. There's people here that have been very good players but have never touched greatness because they didn't have the desire or the passion to make somebody else around them better," he said.

Although the Beavers, like most college teams, rely on pitching to win games or keep an opponent close, Oregon State won its 2007 national title by collecting more than 10 hits in all but its first game in the College World Series. For JUGS® Sports, Coach Casey noted the seven most misunderstood areas in hitting:

- Taking "style" away from a hitter
- Maintaining posture from start to finish for a proper bat path
- Getting movement early and having a rhythm to create bat quickness and velocity
- Getting the stride foot down on time
- Beginning swings with the lower half
- Flowing linearly to angular movement at contact—50 percent centered
- Trying to create extension after contact—should happen naturally

Leadership Lessons

On the Diamond: Simple mistakes are often caused by minor adjustments players make—whether while hitting, pitching, or fielding. Baseball is a game of inches, and players often learn to step a few inches in on the grass for certain players or step away an inch or two from home plate while facing a particular down-the-middle pitcher. You're not always going to get everything to go your way in a game, and working in practice on mistakes that occurred in the last game might seem embarrassing to those players who made errors, but if they work on correcting those errors, they won't be made again—or at least the likelihood will lessen. You can try to practice for every possible scenario in a game, but when a new situation happens in a game and players don't react properly, practice is the best time to discuss needed adjustments.

In the Workplace: Employees don't think about what they do in their jobs as akin to winning and losing, but when they make mistakes, some managers rarely hesitate to let them know. But employees often don't have time in a given day to practice their tasks because they need to spend their workdays actually *doing* tasks. However, managers should strive to offer feedback on their employees' mistakes—in private—and then help them work toward not making them again. For example, for repetitive tasks, such as pulling in data for reports, employees should have a checklist they follow to ensure they're creating an accurate report. But if managers point out mistakes, then employees should adjust that checklist to either add a second review of what they're culling or include some sort of process that requires them to verify certain steps before proceeding with steps that could cause significant errors.

Lesson #16: Keep Fighting
Frank Chance

"The game is never over until the last ball is pitched."

Before Yogi Berra recast this offering as "It ain't over till it's over," Frank Chance's pithy quote expressed how committed he was to playing hard until the last out. And being part of the most famous double play combination in history—Tinkers to Evers to Chance—helped promote him to player-manager when Chicago Cubs manager Frank Selee resigned late in the 1905 season with illness. The players had voted him in, although he had his detractors who didn't like his combative style—especially toward ownership—but his prowess at the plate couldn't be ignored.

Like any player-manager, though, the demands to fulfill both roles with equal aplomb eventually caught up to Chance as he guided the team to four pennants and two World Series titles from 1906 to 1910, which included the Cubs' last World Series title in 1908, but saw his offensive numbers suffer ever so slightly each season until he retired from playing in 1914.

Although Chance could intimidate his players, they appreciated his honesty. From his position at first base, he could easily command or encourage, and players often responded to his dictations. In 1906, in his first season as full-time manager, the Cubs won 116 games—still a franchise record—and the National League pennant but lost to the crosstown White Sox in the World Series. In 1907 and 1908, the Cubs again won National League pennants and then proceeded to beat the Detroit Tigers both seasons to win what remains their last World Series titles.

"It is a delicate thing to handle a team and get the best results," Chance said. "Friendship cannot interfere. Altho a player may be a manager's best friend it is not good business to keep him if he is falling down in his work and injuring the team's chances."

Chance's fierce competitive style as a player and a manager served him and his players well, but it's not a method that might work for everyone. But Chance knew what would work for his teammates because he was there in the trenches with them—and they fought to the end, enjoying more success than any team in Cubs history has enjoyed.

"What qualification, Mr. Chance, above all others, is responsible for your success as a manager?" a reporter once asked.

"My ability to lick any man on the club," he replied, knowing he had earned his players' respect and yet never needed to prove it in a physical way.

Leadership Lessons

On the Diamond: Many teams have entered the ninth inning of a game down by what seems like too many runs and then proceeded to not only score the needed runs but ended up winning the game. A hit here, an error there, a walk or two, an unsuspected bunt, a three-run homer, a triple, a passed ball—the ways teams can capitalize while behind are endless. While players know that the ninth inning (or whatever inning is the last inning at your level) is the last inning, coaches need to encourage an attitude among players that although the score might be 7-2, everyone should think this is the third or sixth inning and that more at bats are possible. Such a deficit might be difficult to drill in practice, but discussing with players their many options when trailing might help them refocus. Your usual course of action during the first eight innings doesn't matter when the team is down to its last chances. Taking risks and utilizing pinch-hitters can help, but it all starts with that first batter. If he can find a way to get on base, then this immediately increases every player's confidence. Just because you didn't do much in the first eight innings doesn't mean you can't rectify that in the ninth inning.

In the Workplace: Most plans have time built in for quality assurance and ensuring that problems and potential errors have been checked for and fixed as necessary. That final deadline isn't always as final as it seems, but an ultimate deadline does exist, and you should do all you can within those limits to help your employees improve a project—as long as no one is sacrificing other projects to their own detriment. In some fields, such as publishing or teaching or accounting, time exists for employees to rectify a spelling error or an incorrect lesson or a calculating mistake. But when someone finds a problem, immediately alert the person in charge of the project. Putting into action a call for addressing that concern will allow someone to take it on—and before a deadline comes or before a product hits the streets.

Lesson #17: Go Big—or Go Home
Ed Cheff

"The hardest thing to do in practice or a game
is not make a big thing out of everything.
Make a big thing out of the big things!"

Ed Cheff served as the head baseball coach for 34 seasons at Lewis-Clark State College in Lewiston, Idaho, where he won nine NAIA national titles, and he currently ranks fifth in college baseball with 1,705 wins. In a 1998 interview with the *Collegiate Baseball Newspaper*, Coach Cheff offered advice about how to organize practices.

"We try to define what the foundation of a good practice is. To us in our program, a good practice centers on a player's total effort and emotion via intellectual, physical and mental terms throughout practice," he said. "Practice is more than just a series of drills and repetition of the bio-mechanical exercise. We try to integrate emotional stability and balance, intellectual appreciation for what they are doing, total physical effort and then have them demonstrate a good mentality. We incorporate those four qualities into everything we do."

He then explained his core elements to practice:

- *Unique drills:* "We have specialized throwing drills where we might have catchers at each base on the infield diamond. Since we have four catchers, we have one at each base. The catcher at first base will throw a ball across the diamond to third while using proper footwork and throwing fundamentals. The catcher at home will throw to the guy at second. Then those players throw back to the other base across the diamond. After a certain number of throws, two of the catchers will snap throw to the next base on the right as the second phase of this drill begins. Then we may go back with the diagonals across the diamond which simulate throws to second again."

- *Batting practice:* "We will face a particular type of pitcher in BP. He might be a soft lefthander or a power righthander. Maybe he is a split finger righthander with decent velocity. Whatever we create will be pitcher specific. At all of our BPs, we try to make it pitcher specific or at least pitch specific. For the first segment of BP, we might have the hitters look at nothing but inside third pitches with fastballs. If we are using machines, it will be 88–90 mph."

- *Shagging balls:* "We have three outfielders who play shallow. Those guys have a competition each practice as to who will make the greatest catch of the day. Every time a ball comes off a bat, it is a contest to see who can make the greatest catch. You are rewarding the effort and hard-nosed mentality of who will go all out to catch a ball. At the end of BP, an outfielder is recognized as making the greatest catch of the day. Your focus as an outfielder is that you work your tail off on every ball that is hit in your vicinity."

- *Practice times:* "You have got to know the mood of your kids. It depends on the time of year. There are so many components to recognize, and you as a coach had better be smart enough to recognize those things. So many times an hour on the field is the best thing in the world for your team. And there are other times when on a Saturday we will practice three hours in the morning, take a break for lunch and then come back later in the day for three more hours in a scrimmage type setting. … If practice takes place right after school, you may have a certain group practice for 1 1/2 hours while the other kids are studying and doing homework in the library. Then the next group can come out and practice the final 1 1/2 hours. The worst thing that can happen is one practice which goes four hours. You have way too many guys you're trying to deal with. Too many guys are standing around watching. Our players are trained to see every possible situation that can come up in a game. And we go over those scenarios thousands of times to be prepared. When a first and third situation crops up defensively, our guys instinctively know what to do because they have worked so hard learning those scenarios."

Leadership Lessons

On the Diamond: What are the big areas your team deals with on a daily or weekly basis—whether in games or in practice—and how do you address them? In baseball, small details have often become too fragmented and the big picture neglected because of situational decisions by players or coaches. How you structure a practice will differ from what might occur in a game because you can't plan for happenstance actions in games. You can practice how to deal with bunts, but you can't always practice for specific bunt placements—try as you might. But if you focus on handling bunts for a certain period of time in every practice, your players will eventually see a plethora of situations they might deal with in a game, and as the coach, you need to help instruct players in developing their instincts based on myriad situations—runners on base, how many outs, and even the score.

In the Workplace: Businesses exist to make profits while also offering a service to people. Those are big things, and you can't always control both aspects simultaneously. What you can do is focus on *your* big thing. You have a role to fulfill, and while your job might come with predetermined limits, don't allow those limits to prevent you from helping with other aspects related to your big thing. Don't neglect your big thing just to help with a bigger thing, but don't neglect your personal and professional goals either. They're not necessarily mutually exclusive, so if you have an idea that can help the bigger thing get done better and perhaps more efficiently, don't hesitate to offer your suggestions. Doing so might just help *you* become a big thing.

Lesson #18: Play Between the Lines
Fred Clarke

"Pennants are not won by managerial hot air or by newspapers. Championships are won on the grass."

While other player-managers might have had a little more success than Fred Clarke, none of them had the chance to play with and manage Hall of Fame shortstop Honus Wagner as long as Clarke did. After combining to win three straight National League pennants from 1901 to 1903 and losing the first World Series in 1903, the duo felt sure they and their Pittsburgh team were the ones to beat in 1908. But after losing the pennant to the Chicago Cubs by a mere game, Clarke offered an impassioned diatribe about his team's heart and the fans' lack of support:

> We have made a good fight, and there is nothing in our record about which we have any right to feel ashamed. ... But the boys did not depend on the plaudits of the multitude, and, they paid little attention to the sneers and criticisms that were hurled at them. They are the gamest lot of fighters it has been my good fortune to command, and I am proud of the way they have acquitted themselves. ... Ball players are not angels. They are not expected to be, but I believe they will measure up well alongside of men in any other calling when it comes to the matter of sobriety, morality and honor. ... They cannot all be Wagners. If they were, no other team would ever have a look-in. But they can all play ball, and they have all done their full duty this season.

Wagner added his own thoughts about the lost pennant and his manager: "I'm awful sorry for Clarke. If ever there was a man who deserved to win it was Fred. That fellow has things awful hard at times, but he never lost heart and he kept us going all the time."

In 1909, Clarke would help the team go to the World Series, winning in seven games against the Detroit Tigers—the one and only World Series meetings between Wagner and Ty Cobb. The Pirates wouldn't win another pennant (or World Series) until 1925, but Clarke had given baseball an exciting team to watch during his tenure with the Pirates. He also developed several baseball-related pieces of equipment: a tarp to cover the infield during rain, sunglasses for outfielders, sliding pads for players, and small bags to haul gear.

Leadership Lessons

On the Diamond: Coaches often try very hard to prevent players from being pushed by media reports, but they often forget how often their own comments can hinder and even hurt players. Sometimes, you have to allow players to make mistakes and then work together as a team to readjust or recuperate from errors. In this way, you'll find out who on your team is a natural leader and who prefers to follow—and nothing is wrong with having followers because they'll be the ones who will do what's needed to help your team win. Temper your calculated criticism with praise and even incentives for when players learn how to play through their mistakes and develop the needed skills to not make them again—or at least limit them to rarity status. But you can't let distractions off the field—parents, newspapers, and unscrupulous characters—determine how your players perform on the field. Let them know you're their advocate. You don't have to be their friend. But they need to be able to count on you for help. Also, never stop trying to be an innovator. One day, your name might end up in a book like this.

In the Workplace: Some businesses are beholden to stockholders and other entities that decide the financial security for those businesses. But you can't continually go about your job with such a heavy burden always weighing on you. While you can't always ignore that pressure, you should focus on what you can do to meet mutual endeavors: helping the company's financial prospects and also enhancing your own. In some fields, such as teaching and law, you're not focused on money as much as you're focused on working within a delicate system that has myriad goals that might not match your personal desires. But when you allow outside forces—politics, protests, and parents—to decide how you go about your work, then you're going to neglect those you're working for. Believe in your charges and stay focused on your collective goals rather than try to suffice someone else's agenda, especially one people might try to push on you.

Lesson #19: Showcase Your Special Skill
Bobby Cox

"You don't have to get hits to impress the manager."

From 1991 to 2005, the Atlanta Braves finished in first place in either the National League West or the National League East every year except 1994 (the strike-shortened season in which the Montreal Expos officially claimed first place). Bobby Cox's team achieved a feat never seen before in baseball, and although the team won just five pennants and but one World Series in that span, most experts agree that those Atlanta Braves teams were some of the best collections of talent ever.

Pete Williams, a former writer for *Street & Smith's SportsBusiness Journal*, summarized Cox's managerial attributes in six succinct adages:

1. *Never speak poorly of anyone:* In interviews, Cox would praise a player who might have had a bad game and would then offer some encouraging words about what the player could do to improve next time. Likewise, if reporters didn't ask about someone he thought deserved acknowledgement for his efforts, Cox wouldn't hesitate to bring him up. This helped Cox develop loyalty from his players.

2. *Pay attention to detail:* When Matt Diaz (DYE-as) came to the Braves in 2006, Cox sought him out to verify the pronunciation of his name. This surely made Diaz feel at home and showed how much attention Cox gave to such details.

3. *It's not about me:* While other managers enjoy extolling their virtues to the masses, Cox remained somewhat shy about expressing his feelings about his own success. He realized it takes more than him to win a game—and more than just his decisions to lose one. It's easy to admire a manager who realizes that baseball isn't an individual sport dominated by its leaders.

4. *I've got your back:* Cox was ejected from games a National League and Major League Baseball record 154 times, but he wasn't known for his fiery temper. What gives? He knew how important it was for players to remain in the game, so he would willingly sacrifice himself to argue a bad call or demand respect for his players. Players become more loyal to a manager who will—pun intended—go to bat for them.

5. *Know how to pick up a colleague:* Dale Murphy offered a story about how Cox helped players recognize that not everything that happens—good or bad—is a result of player achievement nor player error: "You'll come off the field with your head down, having just booted a ball or something. And there's Bobby saying, 'Man, that ball took a wicked hop, didn't it?' You're thinking you should have made the play and you should have. But the point is sometimes it's just a matter of how the ball bounces."

6. *Be consistent:* When Cox first managed the Braves from 1978 to 1981, he was in his early 30s. When he retired in 2010, he was 69. Although he saw baseball change a lot in the intervening three decades, his managing style remained diligent. "He's the same guy he was 30 years ago," said former Braves reliever Gene Garber, who played for Cox in the late 1970s. "He's as consistent as they come."

Leadership Lessons

On the Diamond: What do you do to get your players to notice you? How do you make them feel? How do they react to you? You have to set the standard in your clubhouse and on the field. Making an impression with players will go a long way toward them wanting to play for you as well as telling others about how meaningful you were to them as players and as human beings. You have to incorporate your personality into all your practices and showcase that again during games. Players demand consistency from you as much as you demand it from them. But remind players they can do much more than get a base hit to help the team win.

In the Workplace: Managers love it when employees meet deadlines, but they should also love it when they achieve small successes along the way. Everything has a process. Putting together a proposal or teaching a new concept or even crunching numbers has little parts to it. A final product is a culmination of small yet meaningful wins along the way. Don't force your workers to swing for the fences when a sharp choice or a dedicated attempt at accomplishing a task can get them somewhere just as easily. Remember: Even when they make a mistake, they still did something well because they tried. And that should impress someone—especially you.

Lesson #20: Instill a Spirit

Joe Cronin

*"Boys must have the spirit of competition in some
way and there is none better than baseball."*

Joe Cronin managed the Boston Red Sox for 13 seasons—longer than anyone has managed the Red Sox—while also playing shortstop for 11 of those years. In 1946, the year after he retired as a player, he led the team to its first pennant since 1918, although the Red Sox would lose the World Series to the St. Louis Cardinals. Although Cronin would go on to work as a general manager and as the president of the American League (the only player ever so honored), he left his mark on baseball as a manager and as a shortstop.

During July 1940, in the midst of what would be a fifth-place finish for Boston, Cronin wrote a newspaper article that encouraged managers to persuade players to buy into a manager's system:

The manager must sell his style of play to his players.

Some managers like to sacrifice more than others … play for one run a little earlier. Other like to gamble a little more.

Clubs get farther when the players know what the manager wants, and are for it. There isn't any second guessing.

A manager without the respect of his players is lost. There is a happy medium in maintaining discipline. A manager can be too tough … too strict. He can also be too easy. Extracurricular activities that may do one no harm may do another no good.

Attitudes and temperaments differ, so players cannot be handled alike. Some have to be patted on the back, other kicked.

Coaches can be a big help to a manager … teaching the game to youngsters as he wants it taught.

The third base coach is particularly important. Many victories and defeats can be traced to his judgment in sending or not sending in runners. He also passes the bench manager's signs.

By the end of the training season the manager must decide on what players he can use best, and where.

He must make quick decisions during the course of a game.

He must decide on his starting pitchers … work them in turn … know when to take one out … and have enough pitchers left to work double-headers lying ahead. He must select his relief pitcher as carefully as a starter.

The playing manager plays and hits for everybody. Playing and managing is tougher on the player end than the managing, yet it is a lot harder to manage from the bench. There is something in being in the thick of things. You have the feel of the game.

The manager of a winner has little to do but name his starting pitcher, and that is automatic.

But running a losing club is no cinch. There are a lot of headaches.

The big thing is to have a good club.

Leadership Lessons

On the Diamond: Even if you're a first-year coach or manager, you have an idea about what kind of system you'd like to implement, including how to practice, how to dole out punishment, and how to enjoy a win—and how to work through a loss and its ramifications. You have to do what you feel works for you and encourage your players to buy into your system. You should, though, also prepare to compromise now and again based on your players' abilities and needs, and allowing natural leaders their opportunity to speak up and help out will give you more time to manage the details.

In the Workplace: When you've become a leader in business, you've likely learned some best practices that work well in your field. If you're new to a company but not new to leadership, you might have to take some time to adjust to higher-level nuances. But when you're leading your team, you should encourage your workers to not hesitate to offer suggestions for improving processes but also remind them that some changes might have ripple effects that might keep those ideas from implementation. But once your employees understand a system—including one you've developed and enhanced—then they'll feel better equipped to uncover ways to improve and enhance that system.

Lesson #21: Lead Through Actions
Alvin Dark

"You lead by example."

When Dick Williams quit as manager of the Oakland Athletics after leading them to World Series titles in 1972 and 1973, the team needed a manager who could handle multiple personalities as well as perform his role under the scrutiny of owner Charles Finley. Finley turned to Alvin Dark, who had managed his Kansas City Athletics team in the mid-1960s.

Dark had made his mark in managing as skipper of the San Francisco Giants in the early 1960s—a team that won the National League pennant in 1962, but lost the World Series to the New York Yankees in seven games. That team had several Hispanic and black players, and while some critics believe Dark didn't have faith in their abilities and had some cultural clashes with these players, when he was hired to manage the Giants in 1961, he wrote a letter to the team's star player—and his former teammate during his own stellar career with the Giants: Willie Mays.

"Just a note to say that knowing you will be playing for me is the greatest privilege and thrill any manager could hope to have," Dark's letter said.

"I had never gotten a letter from a manager before," Mays later said. "It impressed me and made me really want to play for him." Dark also made Mays the team captain, hoping he could employ the "Say Hey Kid" as a mediator between himself and those who saw Dark as someone trying to undermine their talents.

"We had more [minorities] than any other ballclub," Dark said. "Knowing that, I tried to get the point across to all those guys, not necessarily in a crowd but individually: 'Hey, listen, I don't care what nationality you are. You have a job to do on this ballclub, and that's the most important thing to me. As long as you do a good job here, I don't care where you came from.'"

While his efforts to that end didn't culminate in a World Series title in San Francisco, Dark did focus on talent rather than nationality or ethnicity when he led that 1974 Athletics team to a third straight World Series title—a feat not accomplished again until the New York Yankees did it from 1998 to 2000. Dark summed up his experience that first season this way: "It's not an easy job to take over a World Championship team. People expect you never to lose a game."

Leadership Lessons

On the Diamond: What actions do your players see you engage in? If you're at the high school or college level, how do students see you in the classroom or in your administration role? If you coach on another level, how do you present yourself publicly? No matter where you coach, though, how you come across to your players in the private setting of a clubhouse or a practice or even on a team bus or plane ride is as important as any other aspect related to how you lead your team. You can prepare them in myriad ways and yet leave them with a tarnished image just through other actions and other words. You might think an action is working with certain players or even the team as a whole, but perceptions might differ from player to player, and that's up to you to control.

In the Workplace: Employees appreciate leaders who can show them better ways and can help them when needed. What impression do you provide your employees with? How do you think they view you? Can you sit down with any employee and help him with his work? Workers appreciate bosses who have "been there" and could do their jobs if needed. This experience gives your employees confidence and also gives them a sense about their own managerial potential and aspirations. Leading by example isn't as difficult as it seems when you're armed with guiding principles that include ensuring your employees see the best of you more often than the worst of you. This approach can also help with morale and employee retention.

Lesson #22: Sell Motivation
Rod Dedeaux

*"First, you have to play smart baseball. If you learn
to do things right all the time, it doesn't matter who you're
playing. Secondly, stay loose. When we work, we work hard;
but we have fun, too. A little clowning always helps."*

In the more than 65 years of the College World Series, perhaps no coach and team have dominated it more than Rod Dedeaux and the University of Southern California. In his 45 years at USC, Coach Dedeaux's teams won 18 conference titles, made 16 College World Series appearances, and won 11 national titles (including an unprecedented five straight from 1970 to 1974), with Coach Dedeaux compiling a 1,332-571-11 record and having the chance to mold such players as Ron Fairly, Tom Seaver, Dave Kingman, Roy Smalley, Fred Lynn, Mark McGwire, and Randy Johnson.

"The things I remember best about playing at USC are that we worked hard, learned a lot and had a really great time doing it," Seaver said. "I learned more in one year at USC under coach Dedeaux than I would have in two or three seasons in the low minors. I learned concentration and to stay in the game mentally."

Coach Dedeaux had three guiding principles to motivating his team:
- Make the person think the way you think.
- Make them feel the way you feel.
- Make them act the way you want them to act.

Leadership Lessons

On the Diamond: Everyone needs motivation from time to time, so when you give your pep talks, focus them on how players can take actions rather than just how players should think and feel in certain situations. Players often have more going on in their heads than just baseball, but when they're playing, you need to ensure that baseball is on the brain. This goal isn't easy to achieve, but taking time to talk with your players on a individual basis will allow you a chance to help your players with their personal problems as well as help refocus them on their performances.

In the Workplace: "Do as I say, not as I do" shouldn't exist in anyone's mantra arsenal. The best way to teach is by doing—"Show, don't tell" being as important in everyday life as it is in writing—and when you take time to show your workers how to do something, they will reciprocate with respect and admiration. If you're just telling people what to do, you'll spend more time dealing with problems than actually getting work done. Showing allows you to not only exhibit a skill, but it also allows you to reach auditory and dual learners rather than merely reach those who learn by hearing.

Lesson #23: Pursue Instincts

Larry Dierker

"A lot of times, managers will say they are playing the percentages. Well, I would defy the managers to tell you what those percentages are. There aren't any percentages on a lot of these things that managers do."

In Larry Dierker's brief five-year career as a manager, the Houston Astros won their division four times, including three straight from 1997 to 1999. That 1999 season was a remarkable one for Dierker because on June 13, he collapsed during a game against the San Diego Padres, having suffered a seizure. He successfully underwent brain surgery and returned 28 games later to helm the team again.

As a former pitcher with more than 100 complete games, Dierker felt that pitchers needed to find ways to get themselves out of trouble and not depend on a bullpen to help them out. But despite having a solid pitching staff during his five seasons, fans came to see the Astros' offense, including Jeff Bagwell, Craig Biggio, and Moises Alou. He preached four key ideas to his team:

- Put together winning streaks.
- Win games on the road.
- Beat the top teams in your league.
- Come back to win games in the late innings.

Dierker took a hands-off approach to managing, and he felt that practice was the best time to help his team with fundamentals and working on game scenarios. Then, when it was time to play, his players could do what felt right to them in any given situation.

"Just try to keep things calm, just try to make good decisions in terms of strategy and be open to suggestions from other people, players and coaches. Don't try to come on like an expert," he said.

Dierker noted that players sometimes take their own instincts and their own habits too far and don't listen to advice from managers or coaches. He summed up why pushing those issues can be detrimental in this way: "If you have a gigantic cannonball that is rolling down a mild slope and that was the team, the manager's ability to influence that would be like trying to push the cannonball on course. You'd be moving it an inch when you want to go a mile."

This doesn't mean managers shouldn't try to influence players or guide them in certain directions, but managers and coaches alike need to assess their players' ability to self-manage, and Dierker had players who could do that, as exemplified by their success.

Leadership Lessons

On the Diamond: Many stories exist that show where a manager put a player into a situation where he got a base hit facing a pitcher against whom he's performed poorly or recorded an out against a batter who has usually dominated him. Just because something happened last time doesn't mean it will happen again, and just because it's happened every time—or nearly every time—doesn't mean a player can't learn to adjust and finally "figure someone out." Statistics and percentages tell but a small part of the story. A good player will best learn how to work through a problem if he can have an opportunity to do so in a challenging situation. Game situations will offer better scenarios than practice because it will deal with the actual combatants. You have to have enough confidence in a player to allow him to work through tough times. You don't get better by sitting on the bench, even though many managers try this tactic and disguise it as giving a player some rest. But why keep a player out of a lineup or a pitcher out of an inning just because of one opponent, especially when he might be able to help your team in other ways—defensively, as a field leader, and maybe as someone who finally resolves his issues and comes through in the clutch to help you win a game?

In the Workplace: Sometimes, a project means a lot to you because of what it will ultimately offer people, and if you become too focused on finances or other numbers issues, you'll lose sight of its potential impact. You can't outright dismiss such aspects, but you can't always feel beholden to them when you know the end result will offer some amazing benefits to people. Weigh the pros and cons, and figure out how to make something happen despite the economical odds.

Lesson #24: Manage With Determination
Leo Durocher

"Managing a ball club is the most vulnerable job in the world. From the moment you take the job you're vulnerable. If you don't win, you're going to be fired. If you do win, you've only put off the day you're going to be fired. And no matter what you do, you're going to be second-guessed. The manager is the only person in the ball park who has to call it right now. Everybody else can call it after it's over."

If it seems like Leo Durocher managed for a long time, it's because he did—managing in five decades from the 1939 Brooklyn Dodgers to the 1973 Houston Astros and winning three National League pennants and a World Series in between. In fact, Durocher is one of the rare managers to lead the Brooklyn Dodgers and the New York Giants, the team he took to the championship in 1954. Thus, he's the only man to manage Jackie Robinson and Willie Mays.

Although he had some great years as Dodgers manager and helped the late 1960s and early 1970s Cubs perform better than they had since the 1940s, until 2010, the Giants hadn't had a team to call world champions since 1954. In that season, the Cleveland Indians won an American League–record 111 (since bested by the New York Yankees' 114 wins in 1998), but the Giants swept the Indians—a series that remains as one of the greatest upsets in sports history.

"I'll tell you, the players make the manager. A good manager can win six, seven, eight games in a season. All big-league managers are different, but we all know the game. No manager is smarter than I am, and I'm no smarter than any of the others. I may gamble where another manager is conservative. But a manager has got to have the right guy on the field to get the job done, no matter what his philosophy is," Durocher said. "I don't give a hoot whether a guy likes me or not. I don't care what he does off the field or what kind of problems he creates for other people. If he comes to play, that's all I ask."

Durocher believed in winning at all costs—even doing what was needed to keep his mother from scoring a run.

"Look, I'm playing third base," he said. "My mother's on second. The ball's hit out to short center. As my mother goes by me on the way to third, I'll accidentally trip her up. I'll help her up, brush her off and tell her I'm sorry, but she doesn't get to third. That's just an exaggeration, but it's an illustration of what I mean. I want to win all the time. If we're spitting at a crack in the wall in my office for pennies, I want to beat you at it. Anybody can finish second. I want to finish first if I can. After that, I've done my job. Otherwise I haven't."

Leadership Lessons

On the Diamond: If you have the opportunity to choose the players for your team, then you'll know what each player can and can't do. Because you've been chosen to coach a team, someone believes in your abilities. While your players might not like some of your decisions and might even make their opinions known, you must ensure players still respect your authority. Whether you decide to handle them as friends or as sons, they still need to look to your for guidance, and you must provide it—as well as offering incentives and repercussions as needed.

In the Workplace: In your leadership role, you have to remain firm about your decisions, but that means being initially open to compromise and other opinions before making solid choices for your staff to follow. People will second-guess you—and you need to allow people a chance to speak up during any part of the process—but you maintain better control of your employees when everyone knows exactly what's expected from him. Your workers should respect that, and when they don't, take the time to privately remind them.

Lesson #25: Don't Embarrass Yourself
Bibb Falk

"You might not be big leaguers,
but you can sure act like you are."

Before Bibb Falk coached the University of Texas for 25 seasons and won the College World Series in 1949 and 1950, his greatest claim to fame had been replacing Shoeless Joe Jackson, who had been suspended from baseball in 1919, in left field in 1920 for the Chicago White Sox.

Coach Falk preached a play-yourself-into-shape approach:

> We did a little of what we called P.T. in the early days, but only when it rained. Other than that the boys ran and threw and played. We wanted long, loose muscles and the word back then was that lifting would tie you up. To be honest I never even heard of a ballplayer using weights. … The key to baseball is power and power comes from speed and we were leery of anything that might slow us up. When I played and for most of my coaching career we always believed that if a man ran enough and threw enough he'd be strong enough.

Although players didn't always enjoy Coach Falk's acerbic feedback, they loved having the chance to play—and win—for him. Coach Falk seldom hesitated to jump into the batting cage to show players how to hit and had remarkable success even when he was in his 60s. Falk's other talent, as it were, was his sharp wit, as compiled by SpikesnStars.com:

- To his All-American slugger who had just hit a game-winning home run to the opposite field: "Are you ever going to learn to pull that pitch?"
- To the infielder who missed a pickoff sign and offered an "I thought …" excuse: "Every time you think, they score three runs."
- To the hitter who had barely missed getting a hit on a line drive that was inches foul: "That's all right—as bad as you are, you may never get another hit anyhow."
- To the relief pitcher who was making an emergency start in the season's biggest game, which also was Falk's final home game: "Go as hard as you can for as long as you can, but don't embarrass anybody out there."
- To a pitcher who took an early shower after being removed during the opponent's ninth inning rally: "You could have stayed out there long enough to see how we got out of the mess you got us into."

Leadership Lessons

On the Diamond: Being a professional means carrying yourself in certain ways. What do you do when your players make a mistake? How do you express adjustments you want made? What do you say when you compliment a player? You can't expect your players to be professionals when you undermine their own development. While Coach Falk's tactics might seem a little confusing and perhaps too honest, he knew his players well enough to know how to get the most from them. What do you do to get the most from your players?

In the Workplace: When you don't feel like your workers are properly representing your team or your company, how do you handle that? How do you maintain a professional atmosphere yet not stifle everyone so much it feels like everyone is in a confined hotbox? How you react to your employees' antics will help define you as a leader and your team within its field.

Lesson #26: Believe in Yourself

Terry Francona

*"Trying to be a little bit better than somebody
else at what you love is a great feeling."*

In 2004, Terry Francona and the Boston Red Sox demystified an 86-year curse by winning a World Series—sweeping the St. Louis Cardinals. In 2007, they did it again—this time by sweeping the Colorado Rockies in the Fall Classic. Red Sox Nation couldn't have been happier. But reversing fortunes after years and years of close calls and miserable teams wasn't easy.

In a 2005 article Francona wrote for *Guideposts* magazine, he explained how positive thinking and faith helped his team win that 2004 World Series:

> I don't believe in curses, not even one that had tormented Red Sox Nation for 86 years. "To win we have to be loyal to each other," I told my players before the start of the 2004 season. "We have to have faith. We have to stay positive. We have to believe."
>
> For six months they had. Now it was October, playoff time. The Red Sox were four victories away from reaching the 2004 World Series and a chance at winning the championship for the first time in nearly a century.
>
> Millions of New Englanders—four generations' worth—were counting on us. All that stood in our way was a best-of-seven league championship series against, naturally, the Yankees, for the right to go to the Series.
>
> What a time to play our worst baseball! We came off the field after Game Three at Fenway Park last October down three games to none. The Yanks had just hammered us 19–8.
>
> The Boston fans were moaning. No playoff team in baseball history had come back from three such losses. I don't doubt some of the fans were thinking: the Curse!
>
> The clubhouse was very quiet. Still, I had this funny feeling and thought, *We can still win this thing.* I eyed each and every one of the guys. "We've won 98 times this year," I said. "We're pretty good at it. Just win tomorrow and we'll be on our way."
>
> If I'd said that to any other group of people I'd have been laughed out of the room. But looking at Kevin Millar, our first baseman; Manny Ramirez, our star outfielder; Johnny Damon, our leadoff hitter; and the rest, I could sense they believed too.

Professional athletes are trained to think positive. In our hugely competitive world it's the only way to succeed. You must believe. You must have faith."

Boston would win the next three games in the ALCS and then win the World Series to end the curse forever.

Leadership Lessons

On the Diamond: One way you can help reinforce positive attitudes among your players is to have everyone sit in a circle and have each player compliment another player—whether on a baseball skill or another attribute. This builds unity because everyone has a chance to voice an opinion as well as learn what others think about him. Do this once a month, keep track of what people say, and reinforce those thoughts when specific players seem down on their luck. But don't forget to add your own positive reinforcements. While teammates' words are helpful, players need to know their coach feels the same.

In the Workplace: Workers are trickier than players in some environments, so instead of a circle, put a box in the office where people can leave anonymous notes about something good other employees have done. Make sure to review these first to ensure people aren't being malicious, but you should also take the time to reinforce these notes with your own handwritten notes from time to time. Your workers will appreciate the effort—and the sentiments.

Lesson #27: Have Fun, Fun, Fun
Ron Fraser

*"Most coaches think winning is all it takes. But it's not.
My attitude has always been, 'Give me an average
baseball team and I'll outdraw your winning team.' If people
come to the ballpark and have fun, they'll come back."*

In his 30 years as the head baseball coach at the University of Miami, Ron Fraser employed different tactics to push college baseball to prominence among sports fans. These tactics have included a fundraising dinner on the infield at Mark Light Stadium, painting bases, having players wear green gloves, and bringing in announcer Mel Allen and legendary hitter Ted Williams for the 1977 regional tournament hosted by Miami. He also encouraged fledgling ESPN to televise college games, which led to live coverage of the College World Series in 1982—and beyond.

This approach worked out well for Coach Fraser because his Hurricanes won the 1982 College World Series—and did so again in 1985—thus saving college baseball and putting Miami on the baseball map. Fans started going to Miami games—and to other college stadiums across the country to see other teams that had started to incorporate more than just baseball into the fan experience—earning respect for a game that had become an afterthought to college football.

"The key word is entertainment, for entertainment is what sports has evolved into and how it must now be marketed, promoted, and publicized," Coach Fraser said. "The competition is no longer simply other sports. These days, sports must be treated as a business, positioned to compete as an entertainment alternative to television, movies, surfing the net, reading, bicycling, or whatever activity people and families choose to do with their discretionary time and dollars."

In *The Baseball Coaching Bible*, Coach Fraser listed his top 10 favorite promotions:

- Attendance record night: an attempt to better the last game's attendance
- $5,000 dinner: eating a meal on the playing field
- $10,000 money scramble: contestants fighting for crumpled bills
- Trip to somewhere: people leaving after the game on an earned trip to an unknown destination
- Open-heart surgery: retirees vying for a free operation
- Lucky numbers: scorecards stamped with numbers that could earn prizes
- Bathing suit day: publicizing a local business
- Lobster bake: feasting on Maine's finest on the baseball field
- VIP suite: opening up space for local and national investors
- *10* night: named after the movie; a player playing all nine positions and DH in one game

Leadership Lessons

On the Diamond: You don't have to go to extremes to promote your program. It's actually better to have events occur before or after games rather than during, although minor and independent leagues have had success drawing crowds for between-inning activities. Your on-field product still needs to be good for people to want to come see the team play. But when you can entice people to do something for charity or for fun, you help build community and allow the team to become a major player in that. This also means doing things in the community rather than always have the community come to you.

In the Workplace: What can you do to make the workplace a little more entertaining without becoming distracting? Can you bring in a string quartet once a month to play relaxing music? Can you have a birthday celebration complete with piñatas and games? You don't have to go overboard to help build unity. The idea is to make an effort—success *can* be found there.

Lesson #28: Earn Respect

Ron Gardenhire

*"We're going to do whatever we can to try to
win games. So pride can go out the window."*

Few managers would want to follow a successful manager, but Ron Gardenhire has done just that. While he hasn't won a World Series (as his predecessor, Tom Kelly, did twice), he has led the Minnesota Twins to six American League Central titles in his 11 seasons. Although that American League pennant remains elusive and patience has started to wane in Minnesota, Gardenhire believes change doesn't come easily—and can't be done just to appease a small few.

"I've been doing this long enough to know that respect is not something you can just go out and buy. You can't go tell them, 'You have to respect me.' You have to earn it," Gardenhire said. "I've been doing this long enough with my coaching staff, and we've had enough success, that I think the players respect that and respect what we do. I think—and this is just me talking—as long as you show players respect, and you go out and put in the effort I think my staff and I do, they enjoy that. I think we have a good atmosphere around here to be successful."

When times are difficult, Gardenhire knows he needs to remain fair yet tough as a manager: "I went through it as a player. If I screwed up a play, I made an error, I struck out with the bases loaded, I expected the manager to be able to say, 'Yeah, he just didn't make a good play.' And that's just as far as it goes. I think the players do know that I have their back. I think every one of them knows that; if something goes on out there, I've got their back."

Twins president Dave St. Peter echoed Gardenhire's sentiments and also complimented his manager on being able to adjust his managing style to suit a changing roster: "I think when you assess employees at any level, whether it be a field manager or somebody within your front office, you have to take a look at the entire body of work. Certainly when we look at Gardy, we look first of all at somebody who has been a part of this organization for two-plus decades and really is an organization-first guy," St. Peter said. "I don't think there's any doubt if you talk to people around the league that Ron Gardenhire is one of the more respected managers in baseball. ... He knows that he needed to adjust some things relative to his own work in terms of the makeup of our roster, of where we are today compared to maybe where we were two years ago."

Leadership Lessons

On the Diamond: When you respect your players and they know they have your support in their intuition—even when situations go awry—then they're apt to do what's needed to help the team win games. When you have players who try to show off or try to put the focus on themselves rather than their attributes or their teammates, you have to temper their egos by giving them a renewed sense of purpose rather than punish them for their antics. You're the manager, so you must show control over your players regardless of the stature of the players or the team's ranking in the standings. Remind arrogant players that such-and-such players could dethrone their positions on the team if they make costly errors or don't perform up to their own self-inflated standards. This reminder doesn't need to be done with a callous tone or in a threatening manner, nor should you coerce players to "help" other players fail. Bad situations will happen naturally, and you should take advantage of them to help all players understand that, for the team to win, everyone needs to realize his role is but one part of the team, not the entire team himself.

In the Workplace: In your job, you can't allow your feelings or attitudes about your employees to color your opinions about their performance. You're in your role because someone believes you can help your team reach its potential. You need to deal with boastful personalities swiftly yet cautiously. Punishment is counterproductive, but a team meeting on how each person's actions impact the team—financially, with consumers, and with other employees not on this team— without pointing out specific people but commenting on specific situations might open some eyes. Change isn't easy, so don't expect it overnight and perhaps not at all how you envision it. But if something good happens, then enjoy the surprise for what it is.

Lesson #29: Know Your Players
Augie Garrido

"We look at fall practice as an introduction to the personalities on our team and a way to get to know the people involved. We are also not trying to defend the National Championship, but instead going out and playing the game, which is a lot easier said than done. We are talking to the players about the importance of enjoying the process without feeling the external pressures of trying to live up to something."

If Augie Garrido coaches the University of Texas in 2013 and 2014, he'll most likely pass Gordie Gillespie for the most wins in college baseball history. He has won five national championships (three at California State University, Fullerton, and two at Texas), and his confident attitude has provided the backbone for his teams' successes in his 40-plus years as a head coach.

In an interview in the *Collegiate Baseball Newspaper*, Coach Garrido discussed bunting, an aspect of hitting that has returned now and again to the college game and one he has excelled at teaching his players. He offered some thoughts about the process and execution of bunting—without putting too much emphasis on consistent success: "Bunting is a way of giving an offensive player an easier way to contribute to the offensive rally. That's my first concern—finding ways to help the player be successful. Bunting is a heck of a lot easier than hitting," he said. "Bunting affects the defensive alignment. The fact that you can bunt brings the infielders on the corners in more often and possibly allows balls that can sneak through that otherwise wouldn't."

Bunting isn't something many players attempt on their own unless they've been given permission to take that initiative. But it can become a game-changing play when executed:

> The first thing to do is have the players understand the value of bunting. Part of the psychological problem with bunting is that you can't simply ask a less than successful hitter to bunt. If you ask such a player to bunt, he thinks you don't have confidence in his hitting, and that doesn't work. The player needs to know that he is bunting because it is his contribution to the rally. Players must practice bunting consistently in game environments and use it in games and not be afraid to do it. There is no question they would rather hit. That's another thing I like about the bunting game. To do it well, it forces the player to be unselfish and make his contribution to the offense when you are advancing runners and so on.

According to Coach Garrido, bunting comes down to simple fundamentals:

- *Choosing an angle early:* "It is important for the bunter to position himself in the front of the batter's box prior to bunting the ball to allow for better bunting angles in fair territory. We have a batting cage that is set up for the bunting game and have targets that the bunters aim for. We also have targets on the field as well when they bunt. We try to bunt at specific areas and try to play games with it so they have fun with it."

- *Balancing the bat:* "I like to see the top hand up on the bat to a point where the barrel is resting between the thumb and forefinger with those fingers out of the way of the ball striking the barrel. Those fingers are firm on the bat. Then you slide the bottom hand up a little bit as well so you have balance. When you have balance, it is easier for you to control the bat and see the ball. Another key teaching point is to keep the barrel of the bat in position so you have the proper angle prior to the ball hitting the bat. Then you can see the ball and the bat come together so that contact zone is out in front of the eyes and slightly off to the side so you don't foul a ball off into your face."

- *Choosing a location:* "A real tough bunt to defense is the one that is in between the pitcher, second baseman and first baseman. If you get all three of those defensive players going for the ball, you have them beat because nobody is covering first base. That is the ideal situation. If the ball is in the right place, it forces three players who all have the responsibility to cover first or get the ball. They all must make a quick decision as to who will do what. That is where the problem is for the defensive players. One must cover the base. Another get the ball and the other get out of the way. It's a tough, tough play to make when the ball is hit in the right spot."

Once the pitcher throws the ball, players should watch the ball come toward them, get the bat in front of them, and then watch the ball hit their bat—and then start running.

"I think what motivated me to teach players to bunt early in my coaching career was that it was a way for the high school players to contribute. For a young player, or any player for that matter, it is about their confidence. If you can't contribute to the offense, then you start playing with less intensity on defense," Coach Garrido said. "It puts the ball in play, and that's one of the major issues with bunting. When you put the ball consistently in play, you have an edge. Bunting allows the batter to hustle down to first base and let the defense make mistakes."

Leadership Lessons

On the Diamond: Even if you don't preach the power of bunting (no pun intended), you must find out how every player—regardless of his designated role or his abilities—can contribute to the offense and the defense of your team. This contribution could include being a pinch runner who can steal a needed base, someone who can pitch in relief in a pinch, or a player who can play more than one position should an injury occur. You learn these abilities through practice, but you have to remember not to assign positions to players based on your own observations. You should take time to allow players to tell you how they'd like to contribute. Then, you can test them on this skill set and keep these self-acknowledged attributes in mind if players show their mettle in their desired ways. And even if a player doesn't prove to you he can pitch, you still know he believes he can, and he might still become an asset in that regard. Baseball is a continual string of processes that lead to runs, outs, and wins and losses. You'll get the most out of your team if they feel like they're an integral part in decisions made related to processes.

In the Workplace: If you're in charge of a small group of people, you'll have an easier time getting to know them and what they can do—even if you hired each person personally. Sometimes, you just have to throw people into difficult situations to see how they respond. But you'll feel armed with strong knowledge if you take the time to get to know your employees and colleagues and have them let you know what they'd like to do or what they could do well. Some businesses don't take enough advantage of their workers' skills, so you can certainly enhance your employer's status if you can show how everyone is contributing to the processes in unique ways and not always aligned with stated job responsibilities.

Lesson #30: Recognize Your Role—
But Don't Let It Define You
Cito Gaston

"I think my job ... is to sort of continue to teach along with manage, and certainly talk to guys about being a winner, wanting to win, and not accepting anything else but winning. I think that's part of my job ... to make sure these kids want to win, play hard, learn something, and continue to teach."

Cito Gaston helped put Canada on the baseball map when his Toronto Blue Jays became the first non–U.S. team to win the World Series in 1992—and then they did it again in 1993. In Gaston's first four years in Toronto, the Blue Jays won the American League East four times—a feat the team had only achieved once since its inception in 1977.

He's also the first—and only—African-American manager to win a World Series. His passive demeanor and power-driven lineups meant not a lot of bunting or pinch hitting, but while this might not have worked for all players and all teams, it worked for a Blue Jays team that featured an eclectic mix of veterans and younger players. In fact, Toronto has had just one second-place finish since 1993, so it's not surprising the team turned to Gaston to manage the team again in 2008. The experiment was short lived, as the Blue Jays still couldn't keep pace with Boston and New York, let alone the surging Tampa Bay Rays and resurgent Baltimore Orioles, and Gaston retired in 2010.

"He's a quiet leader," said Blue Jays pitcher Scott Richmond. "He's not big on the whole rah-rah kind of thing, but he'll let you know when you've done well. He's always preached family first. He made sure we understood this is our job and this is a sport, and that someday you're going to have a tight family to go back to."

"I like to look at myself as someone who always treats people the way I want to be treated, and I don't think I've ever treated anyone poorly," Gaston said. "Maybe you get a couple of guys who don't like the way you look, or don't like whatever and they carried on and people have a tendency to believe what they say. But it's not going to be something I'm going take to bed and worry about."

One catalyst for those Blue Jays titles was how Gaston handled any problems and how he approached leading his teams.

"I think if you treat them like men and respect them like men they will treat you like a man and respect you like a man," he said. "I never had clubhouse meetings or as they are called in baseball 'chew out meetings.' What I would do when one or two players were not playing up to their potential, was I would call them aside and we'd have a one-on-one conversation on what they were doing wrong or what they were not doing. You have to know people. There are some you can scream at and there are some you cannot scream at."

Leadership Lessons

On the Diamond: When you're working with young players who know that winning is the ultimate achievement in baseball, you also have to remind them that "winning" comes in many different forms. Maybe it's returning from an injury and making a quality start. Maybe it's getting a key hit in a situation in which that player has struggled in before. Maybe it's turning a double play on the third attempt in a game. These small victories deserve commendation, and they should come about because you turned a mistake into a teaching moment. And you're not just teaching young men how to play baseball. You're helping them learn skills—communication, teamwork, and compassion—that can serve them well in other endeavors. You can't play baseball forever, but you can be an infinitely good human being. Managing means dealing with the inning-by-inning decisions; teaching means helping others to learn. On some points, these two roles crisscross, but if you teach first and manage second, you'll have much more success—on the field and especially off the field.

In the Workplace: Teachable moments occur almost daily in every field. No matter your personality, use it to your advantage to take time to share knowledge with your colleagues. Never underestimate the power of a lunch-and-learn program in your workplace. You don't always have to be the leader; sometimes, being the facilitator allows your employees to teach something to you. Be open to learning as often as you teach, and you'll have more fun and more successes.

Lesson #31: Delegate Your Authority
Gordie Gillespie

"A coach is in a powerful position with his players.
He should never abuse that power."

When Gordie Gillespie retired in 2011 from being a Division III and NAIA baseball coach, he had amassed 1,893 wins in his 59 years at three schools, putting him atop the list for most wins in college baseball history. Through BaseballTips.com, Coach Gillespie listed these concepts as defensive philosophies that can serve any team well:

- Prevent the big inning.
- "If you hold them scoreless, I promise you a tie" said the offensive coach to the defensive coach!
- We cannot lose if we do not let them score.
- In 65% of games, more runs are scored by the winning team in one inning than the losing team scores in the entire game.
- Pitching is 75% of the game.
- Pitching is 80% of the game.
- Pitching is 90% of the game.
- "Who is the toughest hitter you ever faced?" Anyone with a bat!
- The pitcher is the fifth infielder and protects the center of the diamond.
- The pitcher, when he completes his pitch to home plate, is only 54 feet from the hitter. He better have his glove ready.
- You must be good defensively up the middle.
- All championship teams have a great defensive catcher.
- More errors are made by third basemen than any other position.
- The first baseman makes the rest of the infielders look good.
- That outfield can really go get them.
- Everyone on every play is in the right position.
- They never beat themselves.
- Their pre-game infield practice is really impressive.
- They really play with a great deal of pride.
- Did you see that team hustle on and off the field?
- Keep the runner off first base.
- Keep the runner off third base.

Coach Gillespie also shared with BaseballTips.com these beliefs about being a good coach:

- You have to like young people.
- Teams want organization.

- Sell enthusiasm.
- Practice patience with patient practices.
- Teach persistence.
- Express sincerity and concern.
- Show fairness to everyone.
- Don't compromise your integrity.
- Don't be afraid to show your weaknesses.
- Make writers' jobs easier by being cooperative.
- Take pride in your job as a coach or administrator.
- Acknowledge and admire your coaches' support.

Above all, as Coach Gillespie said, coaches have such a role of authority that it's easy to try to manipulate others into doing what they require and desire, but this seldom works to anyone's advantage.

Leadership Lessons

On the Diamond: Pretend you're a player on your own team. How would you react if you were being berated by your coach? Granted, one reason why some coaches yell is because they were yelled at by coaches they had. Your own personality becomes entangled with someone else's idealized personality, and you can either try to separate the two or remain intertwined with someone who might or might not have had your best interests in mind. You're in a valuable position in a young man's life. You don't have to give him constant gentle coddling. But you do have to remember he's a human being with feelings that deserve your respect, not your vitriol.

In the Workplace: Think about yourself as being one of your employees. Better yet, consider yourself on equal footing with them and carry yourself that way. Tell yourself that in times of need, you're merely the one who should have the answers. But don't neglect your colleagues' answers. They're intelligent people, too. Give them a chance to earn their own credit.

Lesson #32: Plan to Prepare

Joe Girardi

*"A big part of my job is making sure these guys
understand they belong in the big leagues and
they can do it. That's going to be my message, that
just because you're young doesn't mean you can't play."*

Success came quickly and consistently for the New York Yankees once Joe Girardi took over the team after Joe Torre left after the 2007 season. Yankees fans have been continually spoiled by success, but until the Yankees won the World Series in 2009, they hadn't won since 2000—their third title in a row. Girardi came to the Yankees after leading the 2006 Florida Marlins team to a respectable fourth-place finish—which earned him Manager of the Year honors—but then being fired for not doing enough with a young and low-paid team.

Girardi took over a veteran team in New York in 2008 and implemented his usual managing philosophy cultivated from his time as a catcher as well as an engineering student.

"I think numbers are important because I think they always tell a story. But the numbers don't always tell about a person here," said Girardi, pointing at his heart. "About how they're feeling about themselves at the time, and the numbers don't always necessarily tell how difficult it is to do certain things in the game. And I try to draw on my past experiences, things that I've heard players talk about. I never want to forget how difficult the game is."

Past experiences can help a manager know what might work best in any given situation—regardless of what the numbers say. Of course, past experiences don't easily lend themselves to success in future instances.

Relying on his engineering background, Girardi said: "You think about industrial engineers as problem solvers. In baseball, that's what you do. Situations come up all the time where you use the skills you've learned to solve problems. You figure out how to make systems run better and be more efficient, and really that's what you're trying to do as a manager."

But limits to such a philosophy do exist, and managers can counter that through training: "If you think too much, you fail, because the game happens too quickly. The key is preparation. You tell the player, 'Here's the information—now go play.' The data has to become instinctual. You can't think about it in the middle of a pitch," he said. "As a player, as soon as you start thinking a lot out there, you can become paralyzed. I feel like that's the same way as a manager."

Leadership Lessons

On the Diamond: Try as they might, coaches will never fully prepare their teams for all scenarios. Baseball has been around for hundreds of years in one form or another, and the game hasn't changed so wildly that someone—or several someones—couldn't figure it all out, but no one has yet. But you can make plans to prepare for certain situations, and then see how players handle the situations within those situations. You can then use practices to discuss anything that went wrong, but you might never see some of those situations again. But it never hurts to plan to prepare for something and worry less if it does happen.

In the Workplace: Because changes happen often in the business world, managers need to adapt much more quickly than their employees so they can help them through the transitions. You can anticipate problems and create plans to deal with them if they happen, but you also need to prepare to deal with situations you can't predict, which is difficult when you don't know what might happen. But one way to counter that is to have a procedure plan for who might tackle a hardware issue or a software issue or a conflict with a vendor or a problem with a customer. "You learn through experiences" is never truer than when you can't know what you might experience.

Lesson #33: Improve Your Improvements
Charlie Greene

"There is a better way of doing everything. …
Take something good and make it better."

Charlie Greene spent 30 years with Miami-Dade Community College, winning more than 1,000 games, three state titles, and one national championship in the NJCAA in 1981, after which he earned the National Coach of the Year award.

In *The Baseball Coaching Bible*, Coach Greene discussed priorities and strategies coaches should share with pitchers:

- Do not waste a pitch or an at-bat, no matter what the score.
- Practice patience. Do not be in a hurry to get an out. Stick with your game plan.
- Pitching away from the middle of the plate when ahead in the count and toward the middle of the plate when behind in the count. First-pitch strikes are critical.
- Locate the fastball: get the other pitches over the heart of the plate.
- Do not try for a swing and miss with fewer than two strikes.
- Do not worry about the consequences of a pitch. Think of the job at hand. You have no control of other variables.
- Pitch to situations. For example, with no outs and a man on second base, try to stop the ball from being hit to the right side of the field.
- Double up on pitches. Back-to-back pitches stop hitters from guessing, particularly when thrown inside.
- Use the glide step with a good base stealer on first base. Also, change intervals between pitches or hold the ball and step off sometimes.
- Use fastballs when ahead in the count (location) and off-speed pitches when behind in the count (strikes).
- Use an off-speed first pitch with a runner on third base. The batter will be eager to drive in a run.
- Pitch inside when you can afford to hit a batter (open base).
- Use the shake-off signal sometimes even when the correct pitch is called.
- Change the tempo during a long inning. Pick up or slow down the pace.
- Know the balk rule.

Leadership Lessons

On the Diamond: No matter how hard you plan for something—a good situation or a bad one—you might find that circumstances demand a different tactic. Don't be afraid to try something new if you think it might offer a stronger possibility of success than something you've drilled into your players since the first day. Being able to improvise is a core element to success.

In the Workplace: How often do you realize a process isn't working as effectively or as efficiently as it could? Maybe an employee or three have noticed this, too? Work together to come up with a new solution and persuade its implementation. Almost all great inventions have been modified over time to suit a contemporary request or requirement. Don't hesitate to reinvent the wheel if it might help everyone travel a little more smoothly toward success.

Lesson #34: Define Your Success—
And Ignore Detractors
Ozzie Guillen

*"How can you be a choker or a loser
when you've won 91 games?"*

Perhaps no recent manager has been as outspoken as Ozzie Guillen, and while his teams generally perform to his level of expectations—including his 2005 Chicago White Sox team that won the World Series—his humorous no-tongue-barred approach to managing is effective if not somewhat nonchalant. In Rick Morrissey's *Ozzie's School of Management: Lessons From the Dugout, the Clubhouse, and the Doghouse*, Guillen noted his 10 commandments for managing:

1. All men are created equal—in theory.
2. Protect your employees from the barbarians.
3. Promote serenity in the workplace.
4. Get rid of the clutter in their heads.
5. Be nurturing—no matter how much it hurts.
6. Find a mentor.
7. Don't confuse team and family.
8. Play the odds.
9. Manage up.
10. It's better to be the matador than the bull—usually.

"The structure of the book is a bit tongue-and-cheek considering all the 'how to management' books, but I'm not making fun of those books," Morrissey said. "I just thought it would be interesting to turn that concept on its ear. Here's this crazy guy ... and I wanted to take a closer look at how he handles people, situations, and on-field strategy."

Leadership Lessons

On the Diamond: It might seem like 91 wins isn't good enough—Guillen's 2005 team won 99 games, and his 2006 team actually won 90—when other teams win more. But you need to remind your players that they're sometimes playing against themselves and no one else. If your team improves on last year's results, isn't that a goal met? Keep encouraging your players to do that each year. Even a bad year is a great time to develop completely new goals based on that year alone and not a progression from several years. Don't let outside forces—parents, administrators, or the media—dictate your team and individual goals.

In the Workplace: Were profits down this year? What can you do as a manager to encourage your staff to improve their individual numbers? Beyond that, take time to remind your employees that they are their own competition and should have goals that reflect current circumstances, not ones that reach too deep into the past or too far into the future.

Lesson #35: Entertain—and Educate—Without (Much) Reservation
Cliff Gustafson

"In what other game do you get so many chances to visit with your opponent? What's better in life than standing around the batting cage ribbing each other? And what other sport has a statistic as well known or understood as a batting average? You ask any player what he's hitting and he'll say, 'Oh, I don't know. Something like .267.' All baseball is, really, is entertainment for the fans and recreational activity for the players."

In Cliff Gustafson's 29 seasons as the head baseball coach at the University of Texas, the Longhorns won 22 conference championships, 11 conference tournament titles, and two College World Series (in 1975 and 1983). When he retired in 1996, he was the winningest coach in Division I college baseball—a record now held by current Longhorn coach Augie Garrido.

In a conversation with Bobby Burton for Hookem.com, Coach Gustafson explained his version of what's called Gus Ball:

> It's pretty much what they call 'small ball' these days. I believed in good pitching and good defense. My primary goal on offense was to get baserunners. I'd tell the guys to take a lot of pitches. About the only difference between me and some other small ball guys is that I rarely believed in bunting when there was a player on first with no outs. I felt like we were giving up more than a third of the inning when we did that. It was like I was saying, okay, the next two batters have to hit .500 for us to score a run, and those odds aren't good in baseball. Now bunting someone to third with no outs, that's a different story. Getting a runner on third, that's a whole different thought process for me.

> On defense, it was all about practicing everything. We had drills for everything. I'd practice what would seem like really minor things, but we'd do it over and over. I'll give you an example. We used to practice a two-man rundown all the time. Everybody practices the one-man rundown, but what do you do when there are two men on base and one guy is in the rundown? That's the sort of thing I wanted to do. And that ended up helping us on offense, when we had guys on base. We got pretty good at that over the years with our rules and when we did it.

Coach Gustafson also offered some advice for prospective baseball coaches: "I used to teach a coaching baseball class at the university. The thing I would tell anybody who wanted to be a coach is that the most important thing a coach can do is to get his players to play hard for you and for themselves. That's more important than the Xs and Os. … I just felt like I had to get my kids to want it a little more and I had to figure out ways to get them to do that."

Leadership Lessons

On the Diamond: As with any sport, the objective in baseball is to win the game. How your team goes about doing that is often up to the manager and the decisions he makes through the course of a game—but also depending on what players do that a manager can't foretell. You can't easily play a prevent defense or hold the ball to run down the clock. You have to play the game and give the fans something to enjoy. And fans love home runs, but if you have players bunting in odd situations or running against a bad count or taking other risks, the fans will appreciate those chances and even encourage them, although this is more likely when they succeed. But how will you know what might work unless you try them in a game situation? And just because something failed last night doesn't mean it will today.

In the Workplace: Sometimes, you can achieve a lot more through small and seemingly inconsequential actions than grandiose ones. How can you move a project forward and exert a small amount of energy and yet feel like you gave your best effort? How can you promote that concept with your employees? You don't have to hit home runs to have success. Taking chances—ones that have at least been processed via plans and theories about potential outcomes—might serve you much better than constantly trying to succeed through extravagant productions. Whatever situation you're in will dictate how light or strong that risk is.

Lesson #36: Showcase Enthusiasm
Ned Hanlon

*"Players are only human, and when they are compelled to
suppress all noise and excitement, their hearts will go down
in their boots, they will become indifferent, the game
will go glimmering and the public will leave in disgust."*

Ned Hanlon might have started the first managing tree in baseball history when three of his players from the old Baltimore Orioles—John McGraw, Wilbert Robinson, and Hugh Jennings—and one from the Cincinnati Reds (Miller Huggins) went on to have great success as managers in professional baseball. Hanlon and his charges won three straight National League pennants from 1894 to 1896, and Hanlon would win two straight National League pennants in 1899 and 1900 while leading the Brooklyn Superbas (now the Los Angeles Dodgers). As managers, his four stars won 21 pennants (10 by McGraw) and five World Series (two by McGraw and three by Huggins).

"We went to 'school' together in the clubhouse—I was teacher—but anyone could air new ideas," Hanlon said about those Orioles teams. "By pulling the unexpected all the time, we had the opposition always off balance, wondering what was coming next."

Hanlon's contributions to baseball include achieving success with such ideas as the hit-and-run, platooning, fielders covering each other's positions, using a full-time groundskeeper, and scientific bunting. This latter development included the "Baltimore chop," a concept perfected by "Wee Willie" Keeler that involved choking up on the bat and hitting the ball off the ground directly in front of home plate, thereby forcing defenders to scatter to field their positions and also attempt to throw out the runner.

Before Hanlon's final season in Brooklyn, he spoke a succinct thought about performance: "That is the difference between a good team and a poor one—the good one does the right thing at the crisis of the game, while the poor team does the wrong thing and loses."

Leadership Lessons

On the Diamond: If you think everything that could happen in baseball has happened, you'd be wrong. What are some ways you can use to encourage your team to run or score or pitch in different ways? You don't have to resort to tricks to try new tactics. But you do have to take some risks and utilize your team's strengths in trying to achieve success. Some will work, and some won't, and you can't keep doing those that work and discard those that don't. You just have to find the right time to try them again.

In the Workplace: While some processes might work just fine, if you can change some processes to maximize efforts and success rates, why not try them? Granted, you can't try Baltimore chops in your office setting, but you can try to achieve a goal in other ways than those you always have. This might even increase inspiration and morale, especially if employees are encouraged to come up with more efficient ways to complete tasks. Empowerment goes a long way toward giving employees confidence—and a chance to showcase their talents without sacrificing too much.

Lesson #37: Choose Carefully
Bucky Harris

"There are only two things a manager needs to know: when to change pitchers and how to get along with your players."

In his 29 years as a manager, Stanley "Bucky" Harris accomplished several rare feats: He won an American League pennant and World Series with the Washington Senators (its first title) in his first season (1924) as player-manager; he remains the youngest player-manager or manager (at age 27) to win a World Series; and it took him 22 years to return to the postseason, leading the New York Yankees to an American League pennant and World Series title in 1947.

Harris learned tough lessons as a young player-manager surrounded by veterans and described these issues in a 1942 Associated Press article:

> At the start you shake up your line-up and you take chances on players and on situations and the breaks seem to come easy. Later they get tougher and you weigh the responsibility more. …
>
> When I broke in as manager I still had Walter Johnson, one of the greatest hurlers that ever lived, and what I am about to say I say with all respect to him. But I remember my first year, that I used to see Walter weakening just a little bit and I, with the admiration of a kid speaking to his elder, would ask, "Walter, how do you feel?"
>
> And I remember that Walter always gave me the same answer, "Bucky, just let me pitch to one more batter."
>
> Then the next batter would belt the ball some place away off from where we were, and after the first year I learned my lesson.

Leadership Lessons

On the Diamond: When you make decisions, do you allow for player input or do you make choices based on other factors? Some of your players have special talents that assuredly make you feel jealous or ashamed of your own abilities. But those players need support, not a bitter coach who expects too much.

In the Workplace: How often do you have meetings where you let someone else determine the agenda and what's discussed? How often do you sit back and hold your tongue? You're not a manager because you can't do the work. You're a manager because you know how to help empower your staff. Being a conduit can be more fun than being a chassis.

Lesson #38: Enjoy the Experience
Whitey Herzog

*"Be on time. Bust your butt. Play smart.
And have some laughs while you're at it."*

Some managers actually had good playing careers. Others, such as Tommy Lasorda and Sparky Anderson, had terrible careers. Dorrel "Whitey" Herzog was in the latter group, but he turned that negative into a positive as a manager for the Kansas City Royals and the St. Louis Cardinals.

"I was usually one of the poorest players on any team I was on," he said. "And I used to think, 'If I ever become a manager, I'm going to pay just as much attention to the 25th guy on my roster as I do the first.'"

Herzog also gave his players some freedom to do what they needed to do in any given situation.

"The one thing you can't do is keep telling your players to relax. The more you do that the worse they'll get. If they'll just keep running the bases with abandon and playing recklessly, you'll be all right," he said, then added an important caveat about dealing with tough circumstances: "Just do what you've been doing and don't try to come up with anything new."

Of course, as Herzog noted, when you're in a familiar spot, you should know what to do from experience: "A lot of managers will stop taking chances, not wanting to lose the game themselves."

Leadership Lessons

On the Diamond: For one inning a game, allow a player to make decisions for the team. To ensure that every player—regardless of ability—has this opportunity, you might need to do this more than once a game or perhaps you choose situations in games where you ask a designated player's opinion about what to do. To maximize effectiveness for this experiment, give players these chances in practice, too. When players know they have an even bigger stake in a game's outcome, their attitudes will change; hopefully, their self-confidence will go from good to great.

In the Workplace: In very few fields are choices life and death. The world won't end if someone makes a mistake, and the universe won't collapse on itself if you allow your employees to take more charge in the entire team's direction. You're a collective—and that means everyone has something worthwhile to add to the entire dynamic. Allow that to happen frequently, and good results will happen just as often.

Lesson #39: Criticize With Caution
Ralph Houk

*"I don't think you can humiliate
a player and expect him to perform."*

After the 1960 New York Yankees lost the World Series in dramatic fashion to the Pittsburgh Pirates and Bill Mazeroski's unlikely game-winning home run in Game 7, the team fired Casey Stengel. Despite winning seven World Series titles with the Yankees, he was thought too old to continue managing (although he did manage four seasons with the fledgling New York Mets).

Nevertheless, the Yankees brought in Ralph Houk to take over for the legend. With not much change in talent, the Bronx Bombers won the American League pennant in Houk's first three seasons, winning the 1961 and 1962 World Series before being swept by the Los Angeles Dodgers in 1963.

"Ralph learned leadership the hardest way possible—seeing his friends and comrades die around him in the Battle of the Bulge," said Tony Kubek, former Yankees shortstop from 1957 to 1965. "Ralph had a few more difficult times in a leadership position, leading the remnant of a platoon in Europe, than managing a team in a pennant race."

Houk's experiences during World War II defined him as a human being and as a leader. First and foremost, he decided that a firm lineup would help the players be more consistent. But he also didn't want to neglect other players.

"Ralph had a feel for people," Kubek noted. "He spent more time before games with the guys who weren't playing. He'd be in the outfield with them during batting practice."

Leadership Lessons

On the Diamond: You really can get more from a player when you talk with him in private. Embarrassing him in front of his peers will make him self-conscious—and perhaps he feels that way too much already. Don't let surface appearances guide you to do something counter to a sensible action and especially not one that goes against your own principles. Your players will respect you more when you make criticism a confidential affair.

In the Workplace: Calling someone out in a meeting might seem to serve as a warning to other people, but in truth, it might cause everyone to walk on pins and needles around you. You can't have your workers fear you. But they will have a lot more admiration for you when you keep critical assessments between just the two of you.

Lesson #40: Don't Second-Guess Success
Dick Howser

"We expect to win, and that's a good situation to be in."

Before his untimely death from a brain tumor at age 51 in 1987, Dick Howser had returned the Kansas City Royals to baseball prominence. Royals fans had been spoiled by Whitey Herzog's teams in the 1970s, but Howser helped push the franchise to its pinnacle moment by winning the 1985 World Series against the cross-state St. Louis Cardinals.

Howser compiled some ideas about how to be a successful baseball manager:

- *On change:* "Most managers know the right moves to make, but you have to have the players to make it work. If the players don't respond, it's not because of the manager."
- *On confidence:* "You've gotta have a pitcher in the bullpen you can bring in in the seventh, eighth or ninth inning. Most clubs don't have a guy like that … ."
- *On results:* "If I could pick the type of team I'd like to manage, it would be one like ours—good pitching, good defense, guys who can get on base and make things happen. But the key is getting it done, regardless of how you do it."
- *On leadership:* "Anyone can sit in the stands and manage. They can make the decision when to pull the pitcher or when to put in a pinch-hitter. And it's not second-guessing—it's managing."
- *On success:* "I think the manager's main job is to put your players into position to win it. Don't overmanage and take them out of it early; keep them close enough that they have a chance to win it in the late innings. There's no point in having guys running and trying to take the extra base if you don't have the players who can do it."

Leadership Lessons

On the Diamond: Knowing what your players can do will go a long way toward helping them achieve their goals—and the team's goals. But once you know what your players can do and if you find you're missing an element or two, see if you have players who want to learn new skills and help their team in immeasurable ways. Some players will readily volunteer because they know it will mean more playing time. But finding volunteers will allow you to focus on a handful of players rather than reassess the entire team, and you'll know fairly quickly who has the aptitude to fill those holes.

In the Workplace: Some managers like to have strict ways for people to accomplish their tasks. But with people moving from job to job with more frequency than in recent decades, your employees will have been involved in different ways to complete their jobs. Sometimes, it's much easier to let your workers do what they need to do in comfortable ways—as long as they're not preventing someone else from doing the same—than to try to enforce strict regimens.

Lesson #41: Depend on Batteries
Miller Huggins

*"Two things happen to players on a championship team.
First they think they're better than they are. Then when
they begin to lose, they don't know what to do. That's
when the manager has to step in and hold the wires.
That's when the players depend on the manager
more than the manager depends on the players."*

Before Joe McCarthy, Casey Stengel, Ralph Houk, Joe Torre, and Joe Girardi, the New York Yankees had Miller Huggins—and Miller Huggins had Murderers' Row: Earle Combs, Mark Koenig, Babe Ruth, Lou Gehrig, Bob Meusel, and Tony Lazzeri. In his 12 years with the Yankees, the team won six pennants and three World Series, including the 1927 squad that many considered to be the best collection of talent on one team ever.

He might have continued to have great success if not for his sudden death in 1929 at age 51 late in the season. But in 1921, as he led the Yankees to the franchise's first American League pennant, baseball had started to become a different game, caused by alleged changes to the baseball, smaller ballparks, and power hitting. This all meant more focus on pitching and fielding.

In a December 1921 article in *Baseball Magazine*, after the Yanks had lost the World Series to John McGraw and the New York Giants, Huggins talked about how to manage pitching:

> Some of the blame which has been given me has been on my method of handling pitchers. I guess it is now no secret that I have had an uncertain pitching staff. During the close of the seasons I had but two pitchers who could be depended upon to go the full nine innings and that fact was very evident during the series. I have told people that all I wanted was four pitchers, but two is just exactly half of four.
>
> Handling pitchers is, perhaps the most difficult part of a manager's job. Naturally opinions differ on this problem. I have listened to the opinions of my players at times and handled pitchers their way. I am not too set to take good advice or advice that seems to warrant a trial. Then I have handled pitchers my way and it seems to me with better results.
>
> In general there is a tendency on the part of pitchers to complain of overwork. Pitching is a strain I won't deny and the strongest man's arm can get sore with too much exercise. I frankly confess that when I couldn't seem to avoid it, I have overworked my pitchers. ... But the

manager who spends his time in coddling glass arms won't do much else. … The system of working pitchers in regular rotation is good, if you have the pitchers. But if one of my pitchers is going bad I want to put in a better man in his place, if possible.

Huggins also expressed a thought about catchers—the other end of the pitch-and-catch battery—that has proven why so many managers had been catchers in their playing careers: "A good catcher is the quarterback, the carburetor, the lead dog, the pulse taker, the traffic cop and sometimes a lot of unprintable things, but no team gets very far without one."

Leadership Lessons

On the Diamond: When you have leadership from your pitchers and catchers, you'll have a strong infield. Pitchers and catchers need to have awareness at all times about situations and how they can work together to help their teams out of tight jams. Some pitchers and catchers are natural leaders, and you can help your more reluctant pitchers and catchers by pairing novice leaders with innate leaders. This won't always result in stronger neophytes, but it will at least expose them to someone who is a good leader as well as give them the confidence to know that someone can direct on-field decisions as needed.

In the Workplace: Every office has dominant and reticent workers who run the gamut of personalities. When possible, pair up contrasting people to help them feel like they're either pursuing their assets or are gaining new assets or are at least with someone they can learn from. Regardless as to whether inexperienced workers become stronger workers, they at least understand what's involved. And that can make a huge difference in their attitudes.

Lesson #42: Don't Panic

Fred Hutchinson

"The important thing is not to panic. You have to grind, day after day, and forget about yesterday. The easiest thing to do is second-guess, but the worst thing to do is to second-guess yourself. Then you panic."

If Fred Hutchinson had not died from lung cancer at age 45 in 1964, baseball fans might be talking about him as the great manager of the Big Red Machine. And if his name sounds familiar, that's because it's emblazoned on the Fred Hutchinson Cancer Research Center in Seattle, a facility founded by his brother, Dr. William Hutchinson.

But before Hutchinson's untimely death, he helped the Cincinnati Reds become competitive again for the first time since the mid-1940s, including the franchise's first World Series appearance in 1961 since their title-winning team in 1940—a win against a Detroit Tigers team on which Hutch played. In his second full season, he led the team to a National League pennant, and before resigning his post in 1964, the team appeared headed toward another pennant but ultimately finished one game out of first place.

Hutch brought an unusual quality to his manager role: He had been a pitcher during his 10-year career with the Tigers. In fact, during his last two seasons in Detroit, he also served as player-manager for the team. Pitchers don't often become managers because their role on the field is so specific and rarely allows them the chance to get a feel for the entire game. He earned the position because of his leadership skills, as he had been the Tigers' player representative since 1947.

In a 1957 article in *Sports Illustrated*, while Hutch was managing the St. Louis Cardinals, legendary hitter Stan Musial said this about his manager: "Essentially, this team will stand or fall on its young players. Hutchinson is patient with them, knows how to use them. You'll never hear him taking credit. He never does that. But he brings out the best in us, because everything's out on the table with him. Let's put it this way: If I ever hear a player say he can't play for Hutch, then I'll know he can't play for anybody."

Then-trainer Doc Bauman echoed Musial's appreciation: "I'd have to go far back in my memory to recall a finer man. I've seen him leave the clubhouse for a few minutes and stop to ask the clubhouse boy if he could bring back a sandwich. He's got real humility. Some of these guys—and I've seen them—they get to be a manager and right away they have to prove they're big men. They're quick to take credit for anything good a ballplayer does. But Hutch never does that, and these players respect him for it. He goes right on being himself, same to everybody, because he is a big man. I don't know how to say it—he's humble, he's kind, he's strict and he's tough. He's all these things in one man."

While in Cincinnati, Hutch indeed had some young talent to build around: Frank Robinson, Pete Rose, and Jim O'Toole. He helped a young team win games through patience and, in the end, through giving his best because he knew his time left on Earth was short. He didn't panic, but he surely deserved more time to pursue his baseball interests.

"I try to make a ballplayer believe in himself, and the only way you can do that is to give him a chance," Hutch said. "If he plays his way out of the lineup, then you try somebody else. And if you haven't got 'em, you're dead. I seldom read the newspapers. If we won, I know how. If we lost, reading about it won't get the game back."

Leadership Lessons

On the Diamond: Teaching players not to panic isn't as easy as it sounds. Baseball is a quick game, and reactions must come with rapid precision. More often than not, they do. But when they don't, why panic? With the next pitch, the team has a chance to rectify a mistake—and in some cases, it might be that player who made the error. Or it's an opportunity for someone to show his ability to help him team out of a dire situation and figuratively pick up that player who had made the error—whether in pitching, hitting, or fielding. Remind your players about this possibility and how they can erase a problem by refocusing. Also, encourage players to remember that today's goat might be tomorrow's hero.

In the Workplace: Deadlines and demands seem to come faster and faster these days. In your role, you should try to remain focused on priorities and not panic too much when the work keeps piling up. Try to make life a little easier for your employees by taking on some of their tasks when you can. In this way, your employees will see you model managerial behavior and perhaps start asking each other if they can do anything to help each other. When we panic, we're more apt to create more problems and exacerbate those that have just befallen us. Encourage your employees to take a walk, do something mundane but easy to accomplish, or commiserate with others to help build or rebuild their confidence.

Lesson #43: Do Something to Set Yourself Apart
Hughie Jennings

*"The player who never makes a mistake is
the player who never does anything."*

From 1907 to 1909, under Hughie Jennings' leadership, Ty Cobb and Sam Crawford helped the Detroit Tigers to three straight American League pennants—and three straight World Series losses. Despite never winning another pennant as manager, Jennings set himself apart from other managers through his unusual cheerleading tactics, including yelling "Ee-Yah" while simultaneously waving his arms and raising a leg like a pirate to delight the fans; using whistles, horns, and gyrations to encourage players; and even eating grass from the playing field.

Like most former players-turned-managers, Jennings sometimes felt as if his role was to fill out a lineup card and change pitchers when necessary—as they were (and still are) generally the functions of a manager according to the rules. His prime years during his playing career was while with the original Baltimore Orioles under legendary manager Ned Hanlon, where he played alongside future managers John McGraw and Wilbert Robinson as well as "Wee Willie" Keeler, Joe Kelley, and Dan Brouthers—all Hall of Famers. He undoubtedly learned a great deal about how to deal with irascible personalities.

One such personality is the legendary Cobb. Jennings once gave him advice that could have applied to any player: "There isn't anything about baseball I can teach you. Anything I might say to you would merely hinder you in your development. The only thing for you to do is go ahead and do as you please. Use your own judgment. ... Do what you think is best and I'll back you up." When Jennings retired from the Tigers in 1920, he handed the reins over to Cobb.

His days as a player also likely resulted in the inspiration for another pithy gem: "The true leader meets every man under him as an equal, then proves his right to leadership."

Leadership Lessons

On the Diamond: How do you assert yourself as a coach? How do you come across in a manner that's different from other people in your players' lives? What aspects of your personality do you showcase as a coach? How do you cheer on your team, and how do you exact punishments? How your players react to you should help you adjust to them rather than having an entire team trying to adjust to you. Of course, you might think that takes away from your power and influence. But when players can be themselves and you can compromise—in whatever way is comfortable—just enough to come across as a player advocate rather than a my-way-or-the-highway coach, then you'll have a better self-encouraging team. You have to let players make mistakes with some impunity. How else will they learn where they need to improve? You can neither coddle your players nor ignore them. You have to be an integral part of their development, and you can do this in myriad ways. But take note of how your players come across to you.

In the Workplace: When employees make mistakes, this opens a door to opportunity—for teaching, for encouraging, and for adjusting. It's easier to support your workers when you let them do what they think is best rather than having their every movement justified by someone else. Of course, limits to this are important, but the stronger the limit, the more likely that employees will do whatever they want regardless and fight back against reprimands. Employees generally prefer frameworks rather than entire step-by-step directions for how to accomplish their tasks. But as projects progress, you can certainly offer tips on new approaches and then allow workers to adjust them as needed.

Lesson #44: Expect Surprises
Davey Johnson

*"It's my job to make sure everybody
knows what's expected of them."*

During Davey Johnson's time as New York Mets manager, fans expected wins and championships. Fans in his other stops—Cincinnati, Baltimore, Los Angeles, and Washington, D.C.—expected the same. In his 16 seasons as manager, his teams have finished in first or second 12 times—and the 1986 Mets earned him his first and only pennant and World Series.

His teams have generally been somewhat young with only one or two veteran leaders. But Johnson seems to prefer that opportunity to develop a mix of players into a cohesive unit.

"My greatest love as a manager is seeing young players play to their potential," he said. "My job is to create fertile ground for them to develop. That's the sweetness of the whole deal."

Washington Nationals third baseman Ryan Zimmerman observed: "I'm sure every manager wishes he had the track record and the résumé of Davey to be able do whatever he wants. He'll make a decision, and you'll be, like, 'Man, that was pretty gutsy.' It's something a lot of us had never seen before, but it made us more comfortable. He can do something and say, 'Hey, it worked when I won the World Series.' He would never say that. But it gives us the confidence, and confidence spreads."

"You have a manager who's going to fight for his players, the players are going to play hard," Nationals pitcher Edwin Jackson said. "He's not going to cave in. He's not going to bash anybody, but he's always going to have our backs."

After losing his daughter and stepson within the last seven years, Johnson has taken on a new perspective about life while managing the Nationals: "I don't try to relive the past. I'm a looking-forward kind of guy. It's probably the key to the game of baseball for me, too, as a player and a manager. It's not what I'm doing now but what I can do tomorrow."

Leadership Lessons

On the Diamond: Do your players know what you expect from them? Consider offering a brief playbook each week to your players that states your vision and goals for the team—but not individual ones, which should be private conversations with each player—as well as diagrams that explain how they should handle certain game situations. Then, you can spend time in practice going over fundamentals and plays that need strengthening during spring training and then revisit these as needed during the season based on game results.

In the Workplace: While your employer might offer overall goals for its employees, your role as a manager is to ensure your specific team understands what it needs to do to meet those goals. If you're in accounting, you can't be responsible for increasing product demand—and it's unlikely anything the accounting department does will help reach that goal. But when the team is focused on clearly defined goals with detailed processes on achieving them, then expectations can be met. But if people don't know what they need to do, how successful can anyone be?

Lesson #45: Speak From Your Heart
Itch Jones

"I've never looked at it as work. I've always enjoyed going to the ballpark. I've always enjoyed working with players."

Richard "Itch" Jones coached college baseball for 39 years, including 15 at the University of Illinois, and won more than 1,200 games, and he's won more than a half dozen conference titles. In 1990, he earned the NCAA Division I Coach of the Year award, and he was the *Sporting News* Coach of the Year in 1978.

In *The Baseball Coaching Bible*, Coach Jones talked about how important it is to attend clinics—to speak and to learn. This might not seem like an easy task, but it's a worthwhile venture. Likewise, consider it an honor to have someone respect you enough to have you come speak to fellow coaches.

"Good speakers are confident, enthusiastic, make eye contact with the audience, and make each person feel important and realize that he can teach to his team what you are presenting. When you finish the presentation, you want to have inspired the audience to put these new techniques to use with their teams," he said. "You want the coaches to feel that they learned more about the game of baseball, that the time they spent at your session was educational and worthwhile. As a speaker, remember that the coaches pay for the clinic and it is the speaker's responsibility to make it a useful learning experience."

Along with offering the obligatory visual aids, being punctual, keeping the talk short, and leaving time for questions, don't forget an important aspect to any talk: humor.

"A little humor is helpful to loosen up both the audience and you. A speaker often includes some experiences that illustrate a point that he is trying to make," Coach Jones said. "Humorous anecdotes can be a good idea or approach as long as it does not detract from the presentation or take up too much time. ... If you use humor, be sure that it is acceptable to the entire audience."

Likewise, don't forget to take notes, and make it a point to mingle with the other coaches. Being around other people who share your passion will help motivate you in whatever areas you feel you need encouragement.

Leadership Lessons

On the Diamond: Try two tactics within the next three seasons: Host your own clinic and encourage community leaders—not just baseball coaches—to speak at your clinic. Likewise, don't limit yourself to attending only baseball clinics. Many different kinds of clinics exist—take advantage of those in your area or in your state.

In the Workplace: You can increase your employees' knowledge bases by hosting workshops rather than sending people to training somewhere else. Make your company the place people want to go for a conference. And don't neglect people who aren't in your field—they might have something to learn, but they also might have something they can contribute.

Lesson #46: Make a Difference
Dave Keilitz

*"It has been said that the key leadership function
for a coach is getting his players to commit to
something bigger than themselves."*

Dave Keilitz had a short coaching career at Central Michigan—14 seasons as head coach for the Chippewas—but he never had a losing record and won four Mid-American Conference titles. He also earned MAC Coach of the Year honors four times.

Now serving as the executive director for the American Baseball Coaches Association, Coach Keilitz wrote some pointed advice about accountability in *The Baseball Coaching Bible*:

> Young people are impressionable. They will be watching your every move. They want to walk the way you walk, talk the way you talk, and act the way you act. It is said that a team takes on the attitude and characteristics of its coach, and I believe that is true. If you expect to have a classy program, then you must act with class and dignity. …
>
> A coach is expected to instill the best in his players. We take a young person with a certain skill level, and a particular level of intellectual, social, and emotional development, and work to raise all of these to a higher level during the time we have with him. We want to win because winning is normally better for the athlete, the school, the community, and certainly ourselves. But winning is more than just outscoring the opponent. Winning is also helping the people we coach become better in all the areas I mentioned.

Leadership Lessons

On the Diamond: What do you do to help your players understand that the game is bigger than they are? How do you connect baseball to life? How do you show parallels between baseball lessons and life lessons? Remember, you might coach a player—or several—who become coaches. When you attend their games, what impressions do you hope they showcase that they learned from you?

In the Workplace: Not every employee endeavors to become a manager, but in small ways, everyone is leader or role model to someone else. How do you carry yourself in front of your employees and colleagues? If one of your employees gains a position in another department in the company, what kind of role model will that person be, and what did you offer that person that he now exhibits?

Lesson #47: Remember Your Support

Tom Kelly

*"I think you need these little reminders of
what you've gone through to get to this level."*

Within a short five-year period, Tom Kelly helped an entire franchise erase years of misery when he led the Minnesota Twins to World Series titles in 1987 and 1991. Not since the team was in Washington, D.C., had it won a World Series (doing so just once—in 1924 as the Senators).

"My players make me look smart or stupid. I just try not to screw things up," he said. "You've got to have the horses to go to the post. There's an unwritten book you're supposed to play by. Well, you better recognize on your own what you're supposed to do to win a ball game."

Kelly often deflected focus away from himself, and instead preferred to talk about his players. In his mind, they were the ones doing the hard work.

"Tom Kelly has a simple code," said former Twins general manager Andy MacPhail. "He demands three hours of the players' attention and hustle. Not for himself, as I see it, but out of respect for the game. When a player shows respect for the game, Kelly shows respect for the player. Remember, he wouldn't even go out on the field in '87 because he thought it was the players' moment."

In fact, while his players celebrated on the field at the Metrodome, Kelly hugged the assistant clubhouse manager, expressing his thanks for the "little people" who truly make an organization run smoothly.

Leadership Lessons

On the Diamond: When the season ends and you have an awards banquet, don't forget to show appreciation for parents, siblings, teachers, friends, support staff at your school, and those people who help your team travel from place to place as well as accomplish other tasks for your team. Some appreciative tokens might include signed baseballs, framed team pictures, gift cards, a placard with thank-you notes from the players, and even baked goods. Everyone enjoys being rewarded for being part of something regardless of the intended outcome.

In the Workplace: No matter what roles people fill in your work setting, don't neglect their contributions. Sometimes, they're the ones who are ultimately responsible for a shipment arriving on time, a phone call being placed at the right moment, and even ensuring a deadline is met. Remember: Small tokens can prove quite meaningful, and they will often give someone the confidence he needs to know he has done a good job.

Lesson #48: Life Exists After—and Beyond—Baseball

Jerry Kindall

"There's a subtle danger that a coach must avoid: fostering an attitude of complete concentration in baseball. It would be tragic to allow an athlete to become so narrow in his life's philosophy that baseball was all he lived for."

Jerry Kindall played for legendary baseball coach Dick Siebert at the University of Minnesota and then helmed the University of Arizona from 1973 to 1996 after a nine-year career as an infielder with the Chicago Cubs, Cleveland Indians, and Minnesota Twins.

Coach Kindall led the Wildcats to College World Series titles in 1976, 1980, and 1986, won more than 800 games in his 24 seasons, and earned three Coach of the Year awards. In *The Baseball Coaching Bible*, which he edited with legendary coach John Winkin, Coach Kindall offered advice on how coaches can prevent burnout:

- *Have realistic expectations:* "I believe that it is a gift in coaching to look at the bright side of things. But that attitude must be tempered by pragmatism and a realistic evaluation of the many variables we face each year with our teams. Most notable among these variables is talent—how good are the players?

- *Recognize and respect authority:* "Those of us in coaching often find ourselves unhappy and bristling with our superiors for reasons real and imagined. This will cause an uneasy and sometimes adversarial relationship with that important person or persons. … Let's do the best we can with a happy heart and a smile on our face. Not only will we be more at peace with our jobs, we will gladden the hearts of our players, associates, and most important, our families."

- *Use and trust your associates:* "My first heading coaching job was at the University of Arizona. … I felt I knew the game well enough, but I was not very well prepared for the host of other responsibilities thrust upon me—budget construction and control, public relations, promotion of the program, recruiting, raising money, hiring a staff, alumni needs and concerns, and more. Further, I felt personally responsible to be the lead in every area of the game—pitching, hitting, base running, fielding, team offense and defense, team rules and requirements, and so on. Besides that, I handled all travel, meals, and hotel arrangements. In retrospect, I see how that I not only created a monster for myself but inadvertently overlooked the extraordinary talents and abilities of my assistant coaches."

Leadership Lessons

On the Diamond: Never forget that your players have more going on in their lives than baseball practices and games. But keep this in mind for yourself, too. Allowing players to have fun by engaging in their own hobbies will prevent burnout and disenchantment—and this also goes for you. Too often, teams are right back at practice after a season ends. Why? Let last season go, and allow everyone to enjoy a healthy off-season. Plenty of time will exist later for practice and training.

In the Workplace: Workplaces have become better at recognizing workers' needs in terms of their families and other activities they're involved with. Some even help foster relationships with community entities. You likely have your own pursuits you wish to enjoy when not working, so finding ways to allow everyone to go home at the usual hour will cut down on turnover and will help increase morale.

Lesson #49: Step Up Your Game
Stuart Lake

"A winning ballplayer puts the team above himself."

Stuart Lake, the current head baseball coach at Charleston Southern University, has coached more than 75 players who have played at the professional level. He earned Big South Coach of the Year honors in 2011 after leading the Buccaneers to a 12-win improvement from 2010.

Coach Lake expanded on some thoughts about what he looks for in high school players and how players can make adjustments to the collegiate game:

- *On gaining attention:* "Emphasize what your strengths are on the field. With that being said, how a player carries himself on and off the field and how he respects the game is essential."

- *On earning respect:* "There are a lot of high school coaches that are still passionate about playing the game the right way, but I see the lack of respect at the high school level. With that being said, I work through it and find the guys who respect the game, their coaches, umpire, etc. You can find those guys."

- *On recruiting players:* "I love guys who seem to field the ball in their glove every time. Not on the end of their glove or the heel of their glove. But the biggest thing is the slow roller. If I'm recruiting an infielder, I want to see him field a slow roller to see how he controls his body and makes the throw."

- *On making adjustments:* "Nowadays, I notice that [freshmen are] treated different by their parents and coaches than I was when I was a kid. The freshmen will get to college and look to me to help them find their classes instead of stepping up and taking the initiative themselves. With that being said, we have to take care of them because that's what us coaches are there for—to develop young men."

- *On impressing the coach:* "Show up every day early. Get there early if you want to be noticed. Stay there a little late getting some extra work in. Another great way, get above a 3.0. Academics do not go unnoticed. I've had the privilege to learn from some of the great coaches. Do the little things. Rake a baseline—just do the little things that let people know that you care."

- *On elevating your game:* "Just love the game. Don't make it a job or feel like you're being forced to play the game. I say this to aspiring ballplayers all the time, 'Play this great game of baseball as long as you can and when they tell you "You can't play anymore," find a job.'"

Leadership Lessons

On the Diamond: You have to recognize the fine line between coach and babysitter. Some players might see you as a father figure, but you can't fulfill that familial role for them because it will stretch you thin. You can, of course, model good behaviors and attitudes and have expectations that they return those traits to you in how they treat you. But your top priority should be to offer tools to players and let them make the best use of them. This isn't to say you can't be involved in your players' lives. You certainly can and should. But you have to have established boundaries for how much you can and will do for them.

In the Workplace: Your workers aren't your children nor are you their parent. You can't solve all your workers' personal problems—if any—but you can offer them tools to help them with their professional responsibilities. You shouldn't neglect their personal needs, but unless they come to you—showing they trust you—you can't always offer help to them without their asking. Just remember to set limits for what you're willing to do.

Lesson #50: Focus on Attitude
Tony La Russa

*"If you want to be a loser, there's always a way
to dwell on the negative. If you want to win,
there's always a way to think positively."*

Whether you love him or hate him, Tony La Russa is a winner. In fact, he's the third-winningest manager in baseball history. His fierce Oakland Athletics and his dominant St. Louis Cardinals won six pennants and three World Series in his 26 seasons spent guiding these two teams, and he's the second of two managers (Sparky Anderson being the first) to win a World Series in both leagues.

Known as a micromanager, La Russa prefers to focus on all the minute details that any given game might have, but he doesn't like to think of himself as the true catalyst to his team's success and downplays having such characteristics that would result in a make-or-break team.

"I don't really think coaches and managers have attributes," he said. "I think what you do is, you have to be in good situations and then you try to not take them for granted and create—along with your coaches and other members of your organization—the healthiest, most positive environment for players to grow and produce."

Although baseball has evolved some since La Russa's first managerial job with the Chicago White Sox, today's climate continues to thrust players into tricky situations.

"I would say the biggest challenge is having players fight through the distractions and concentrate on true professionalism, which is best effort to learn what the craft is about and best effort against the competition," he added. "Players today get too distracted by the chance to make money, so they chase statistics and attention. The media is driven by, in many cases, the controversy. Which is what sells. Not the basics. So players really need to fight through all of that and really stress being as good a professional as they can be and the rest of the stuff falls in place."

La Russa also believes that getting to know your players can help foster a team that understands it is, in fact, a team, not an individual sport where personal goals are more important than team chemistry or team success.

"Our staff, we believe in being very personal, up-close with our players," he said. "It's not a line drawn and you rarely step over it. We really believe in a lot of intermingling and making each other personally accountable to each other. In other words, you care for your players. Actually, it's a harder way to lead, because you spend a lot of time as a staff thinking about each and every guy, every day."

Leadership Lessons

On the Diamond: A theory in psychology says if someone berates you and you become angry about it, then that's on you, not the aggressor. You can control your thoughts and emotions and how you react to such an action. This is equally true in baseball. Just because things are going poorly doesn't mean they'll continue that way; sadly, this is also true for when things are going well. But how you deal with disappointments and achievements can define your team's ability to deal with these extremes. You should show compassion toward your players as well as not allow celebrations to interfere with the next goal because just as easily as a negative can become a positive, a positive can become a negative, especially when expectations become too high and players are trying too hard to perform to a standard that might have been an anomaly.

In the Workplace: You have to be a guiding light to your employees when times are tough, and you also need to cautiously temper their enthusiasm when success attempts to overwhelm. And tough times will likely happen, but how can you turn that into a positive? It can't just be "Well, we're still here and have jobs, so we should be thankful." It has to be something more akin to "We're in a tough spot, but we can join together to get work done as efficiently as ever—and here's how." Then, break down problems into small groupings and tackle the higher-level crises first so not-so-tough issues will seem easier in comparison. Of course, you can also build confidence through doing easy tasks first, but this depends on your team's morale.

Lesson #51: Befriend Your Players
Tommy Lasorda

"I motivate players through communication, being honest with them, having them respect and appreciate your ability and your help. I started in the minor leagues. I used to hug my players when they did something well. That's my enthusiasm. That's my personality. I jump with joy when we win. I try to be on a close basis with my players. People say you can't go out and eat with your players. I say, why not?"

Perhaps no manager has offered a more charismatic and passionate approach to managing than Tommy Lasorda, but don't let that soft exterior hide his fiery attitude about how to play baseball. In a 1989 article in *Fortune* magazine, Lasorda explained how he saw his role as manager:

I can remember when I was 15 years old. I was sitting at home in the kitchen and my mother had a can of Carnation milk. I'll never forget this. A little can sitting on the table, and I picked it up, and why I ever read what was on that can I'll never know. It had a slogan on it, and it says contented cows give better milk. And I believe that contented people give better performances.

How do you get contented people? I want my players to know that I appreciate what they do for me. I want them to know that I depend on them. I define a leader as someone who walks out in front of his men but he doesn't get too far out in front to where he cannot hear their footsteps. When you as a leader of people are naive enough to think that you, not your players, won the game, then you're in bad shape. Because when you start believing that, what happens? You become too wrapped up in your own importance.

You have to show you care? Well, you gotta talk to them. You gotta communicate with them. I take them out and work with them. There's no set way of doing the thing. See, I believe in hugging my players. I believe in patting them on the back. See, I believe in motivation. People say, God, you mean to tell me you've got a guy making a million and a half dollars and you got to motivate him? I say, absolutely. Everybody needs to be motivated. Everybody from the President of the United States on down to the guy who works in the clubhouse. We need to be convinced that we can do better than we're doing. That's where motivation becomes important. It's not a question that you're lazy. It's that you think in your mind, in your heart, that you're doing the best you can, but you're really not. If I can extract from all of the players all of the abilities that they have within them, then they're going to be tough to beat.

This approach helped Lasorda take over for legendary manager Walter Alston and continue the Dodgers' dominance in the National League by leading Los Angeles to four pennants and two World Series titles in his 21 seasons. But as Lasorda readily admits, success doesn't come just because players have talent and they're surrounded by talent: "You have to believe in yourself before others can believe in you."

Leadership Lessons

On the Diamond: You don't have to be best friends with all your players to be friendly with them. Treat them as you request they treat you. Yes, some coaches seem to love yelling at players or embarrassing them, but they wouldn't stand for that from their players. It's hard to argue with those coaches who have had success on the field and were known as yellers. But will your players respect you in 10, 20, or 30 years? Or will they admire your coaching abilities and nothing else? Take your team out to dinner once every other week and notice how they change in how they carry themselves in practices and in games. Meet with their families. Meet their girlfriends and wives. Take an interest in them as human beings, and you should notice them taking more of an interest in you. Be a leader and be a teacher, but be a friend first.

In the Workplace: Some managers were once employees who worked and sweated with the colleagues they now lead. You can't just let those relationships go because of a change in roles. If the previous manager engaged the staff in certain activities, keep those up to maintain consistency and minimize dissention; if not—and if the staff did things on its own with an engaged manager (or maybe even in spite of an engaged leader)—then take the time to do things as a group outside work that will keep friendly vibes going. You'll get a lot more out of people if they can trust you because you're willing to go out to a movie as a group or attend a community event as a team.

Lesson #52: Coach for Success

Jack Leggett

"Our daily goals are to play at a national championship level. We strive to exhibit the discipline necessary in everything we do, both on and off the field, to win the national championship. We talk about it—we don't hide it."

Jack Leggett is the current head baseball coach at Clemson University, and in his 17 years, he has won more than 750 games, taking his team to the NCAA tournament 16 times and leading the Tigers to six College World Series appearances. He has also earned Atlantic Coast Conference Coach of the Year honors three times.

One aspect Coach Leggett likes to discuss is how successful players are coachable:

- They want to learn, so you have to teach.
- They think they're tough mentally and physically, so you have to challenge them.
- They're competitive in everything they do, so you must compete.
- They're consistent in everything they do, so you must repeat.
- They need to work hard, so you have to push their limits.
- They love to win, so you must play to win in practice.
- They should hustle, so you must expect hustle in practice.
- They need discipline, so you must demand excellence.

To these ends, he establishes team goals:

- Making promises
- Developing and improving players
- Developing mentally and physically tough players
- Pursuing a competitive spirit and attitude
- Developing a tradition (academics, dress, plate)
- Having a great hitting team
- Having a hustling team
- Demanding excellence, discipline, and perfection in practice
- Putting a stamp on the team
- Paying attention to details
- Finishing off games
- Getting what you ask for
- Having a great pitching and defensive team
- Developing teamwork/unselfishness
- Developing baserunning and pressure games on offense

Leadership Lessons

On the Diamond: Team goals are vital to keep everyone focused on a collective goal. But don't forget to establish personal goals for each player. In fact, each player should write up his season goals and then compare them with yours for him. But his list should also include one goal he has for you as coach. Don't think you can't learn from your players. You do. All the time. Make a more conscious effort to learn from them this season.

In the Workplace: In most business environments, workers have to come up with goals for the next fiscal year. Some are given to them from corporate headquarters or a more local entity, including an internal unit. Usually, they can come up with a handful for themselves, but you should also offer some for them to achieve. Likewise, encourage your employees to come up with some goals for you. It's not just about improvement. It's also about showing that you're part of the team and willing to put in as much effort as your workers.

Lesson #53: Forget Mind Games
Jim Leyland

"We need to have preparation to win. A disciplined team will win more closer games over a period of time."

Whether managing in Pittsburgh or Florida or Colorado or now in Detroit, Jim Leyland has brought his own special style to the position. Like many managers before him, he learned the game through playing, but he also learned valuable lessons as a Minor League manager, which, strangely enough, he did in the Tigers' organization.

"The one thing I decided to do from the beginning was to be honest," Leyland said. "That is the most important thing. Be honest. Tell a guy what you really think about him. He might not like it, but if he knows you're honest, he has to respect you. You start playing games with people and you're lost."

Late in the 1990 season, as the Pirates headed toward its first of three straight National League West division titles, Leyland spoke a comment that has become a true prediction for all his future teams.

"I'm not a great believer in momentum or any of that," he said. "I think that your momentum is as good as your next starting pitcher. Talent is what is important, and this club has talent—a lot of talent. What I want are guys who can grind it out day after day and not fluctuate."

Leadership Lessons

On the Diamond: Lies are hard to remember. Why play games with your players when you can offer straightforward suggestions and gain straightforward results in return? Players will more easily rectify their errors if you're firm in your feedback. Don't be wishy-washy like Charlie Brown. Be resolute like Lucy Van Pelt.

In the Workplace: Sometimes, managers know information they're not supposed to share with their employees, but as often as you can, letting your workers know where things stand will allow them to relax and go about their work in a confident manner. If workers feel or detect that you're not being upfront with them, they will lose respect, and this can't end well for team commitment and spirits.

Lesson #54: Reflect Your Best
Danny Litwhiler

"Do anything that gives you confidence or a positive image of yourself. Always see yourself to be successful in the mirror of your mind. Never see yourself fail. This is a drill of the mind."

Danny Litwhiler lived quite an exciting life—from being a Major League player to playing in two World Series to being just the third baseball coach at Florida State University. In his 28 years at FSU and at Michigan State University, he won 678 games and led his teams to nine NCAA tournament appearances and three trips to the College World Series.

In *The Baseball Coaching Bible*, Coach Litwhiler discussed conditioning—an integral aspect to ensuring players have physically prepared themselves to perform:

Besides using off-season drills, players should participate in other sports or activities. One of the best is handball or paddleball, using the glove or paddle to hit the ball with the fielding hand. This develops dexterity with the glove hand of baseball.

Running, tennis, Ping-Pong®, soccer, jumping rope, and swimming are all good activities for maintaining physical condition. Swimming develops the shoulder muscles. Using the overhand stroke develops muscles almost identical to those used in throwing a baseball. But players should keep throwing a baseball between swimming sessions. Tennis and Ping-Pong are good for the batting eye. Basketball, tennis, and running are good for developing leg strength and lateral movement. Many major-league players were good basketball players. Football as a conditioner for baseball is not recommended because of the obvious possibility of injury, which could damage a baseball career. …

Preparation for a baseball season requires players to work on their own, physically and mentally, from the last game of the previous season until the first day of official practice. At a minimum, players should work on their own for at least a month before the spring-training opening.

Leadership Lessons

On the Diamond: Once the season starts, practices might take on a different feel. Playing games will keep players in good condition, but it might be good to engage your team in some fun yet physically demanding activities that will help them maintain focus while also continuing to develop their baseball skills. Something as simple as lawn darts or croquet or as challenging as bowling or even water polo will push your players to reconsider their postures as well as allow them to contemplate how to achieve baseball-related goals in other sports, such as hitting a target or putting a ball through a narrow hoop.

In the Workplace: Ergonomics has become quite a buzzword these days, and you should do all you can to ensure your employees are in good physical condition relative to the demands of their jobs. But it wouldn't hurt to pamper employees now and again, such as with 15-minute massages by a professional, maybe more comfortable chairs, and, of course, doing something fun as a group after work. This approach will help your employees relax more and feel less pressure when they know something good is coming their way.

Lesson #55: Extend Your Passions
Al Lopez

*"Do what you love to do—and give it your very best.
Whether it's business, or baseball, or the theater,
or any field, if you don't love what you're doing and
you can't give it your best, get out of it! Life is too
short! You'll be an old man before you know it."*

From 1949 to 1964, the New York Yankees won the American League pennant every year except 1954 and 1959—and Al Lopez's teams were the ones to keep them from 16 consecutive pennants, including a then-record 111 wins by Lopez's 1954 Cleveland Indians. In fact, in Lopez's first 10 years as a manager (six with Cleveland, and four with the Chicago White Sox), his teams never finished below third place, and in his 15 full seasons, his teams never won fewer than 82 games.

Like many managers before and since, Lopez honed his skills as a catcher. He played almost his entire career in the National League, and bringing that knowledge to the American League gave him different options when managing his teams.

"He knew about catching, he knew about defense, he knew about pitching," former Indians third baseman Al Rosen said. "He was one of those people who just had a great feel for the game. I think every player who ever played for him must feel the same way: He was the consummate gentleman, and you knew he was always in your corner."

Lopez learned a great deal from his former managers—including Hall of Famers Wilbert Robinson, Casey Stengel, Bill McKechnie, Frankie Frisch, and Lou Boudreau—but also brought his own personality to his job, earning him the nickname El Señor.

"He was very fair," former White Sox outfielder Jim Rivera said. "If you did something good, he would compliment you. If you struck out or made an error, he wouldn't say a word as long as you hustled and worked hard."

"Managing can be more discouraging than playing, especially when you're losing, because when you're a player, there are at least individual goals you can shoot for," Lopez said. "When you're a manager all the worries of the team become your worries."

Leadership Lessons

On the Diamond: Life *is* short, but if you love coaching baseball, keep doing it in whatever way you can. If you love baseball, you'll find ways to stick around the game. You can't force players to have the same passion you have, but you can impress upon them how important it is to have a passion and to not merely follow that love, but to lead that love and have it work for them. Sometimes, all you need is a small dream and a little encouragement—the rest is up to your effort.

In the Workplace: It won't take long for you to discover your employees' passions, but once you're aware of them, do what you can to encourage them and give employees more of an ability to pursue them. Life *is* short. Allow people to make the most of whatever time they have.

Lesson #56: Analyze Characters
Andy Lopez

*"I truly believe that our most important challenge in
coaching, above and beyond the wins, is the attempt
to establish the winning character in every young man
we coach while always focusing on this statement:
'One man with character is going to equal the majority.'"*

When the University of Arizona won the 2012 College World Series, Andy Lopez became just the second college baseball coach to win the prestigious title with two different schools, having previously led Pepperdine to the title in 1992 (by beating California State University at Fullerton, which was then coached by the other man to earn such an honor: Augie Garrido, who won College World Series titles at Cal State Fullerton and at the University of Texas). He has also won seven conference titles and three National Coach of the Year awards.

In *The Baseball Coaching Bible*, Coach Lopez laid out what he believes are characteristics for success:

- *Confidence:* This comes from preparation, focusing on details, and forming strong work habits.
- *Persistence:* Even when barriers seem to mount up, being able to overcome them—and even enjoy and appreciate the struggles—can lead to victories down the road.
- *Courage:* Confront weaknesses and gain experience from fighting them, which can lead to success in future situations.
- *Poise:* Life is about trying to find that middle road—that balance between winning and losing. This also includes working at your own pace and taking control of emotions and thoughts.
- *Perspective:* Achievement in this moment is fleeting. More moments will come to test yourself, and you can define yourself in that instance and then let go—win or lose.
- *Loyalty:* Being selfless and focusing on specific goals will help players play as a team and for the team rather than for individual accolades.

Leadership Lessons

On the Diamond: Confidence and character are tough to build up but easy to take away from a player. You can encourage a player with a difficult personality to do for the team and yet not change his entire mindset by reminding him that in this moment, he has a chance to do something great for his team that will also reflect who he is. Coaches would love for players to conduct themselves the same way all the time, but does anyone ever do this? They try, but it's not as simple as it seems. Thus, it's better to keep players focused on team goals and then allow them whatever freedom they need to be the people they want to be in other areas in their lives. The hope for such challenging players is that baseball character will permeate into their lives.

In the Workplace: People carry themselves differently at work—and likely adhere to different rules—than they do at home or in their personal lives. It's best to remind employees they can do what they want to do outside the office, but that they need to at least travel a safe line at work. This makes the work environment better for all employees. Remember, it's easier to ask one person to modify his ways and/or compromise his beliefs than to ask an entire team to make changes to accommodate one or two selfish people.

Lesson #57: Empower Yourself
Connie Mack

"Humanity is the keystone that holds nations and men together. When that collapses, the whole structure crumbles. This is as true of baseball teams as any other pursuit in life."

Cornelius McGillicuddy Sr. proved that if someone wants to manage a baseball team at age 87, he should surely be allowed to do so. He also proved that numbers lie. When the American League claimed Major League status in 1901, joining the National League as a second circuit for professional players, the Philadelphia Athletics franchise began as competition for Philadelphia Phillies fans. Enlisted to manage the team, Connie Mack bought a 25 percent interest in the Athletics and would helm the team for 50 years. He had previously been a player-manager for the Pittsburgh Pirates for three years, but his greatest achievements came with the Athletics.

During his 50-year tenure with the A's, he won 3,582 games and lost 3,814 (putting him at 3,731-3,948 for his career, setting records that still stand for most wins and most losses by a manager), but his teams won nine pennants and five World Series. Mack usually recruited players from college teams because he knew they would come to the team with experience and perhaps a little knowledge about how the world works.

According to historian Bill James, Mack knew what he needed in a player: "Mack looked for seven things in a young player: physical ability, intelligence, courage, disposition, will power, general alertness and personal habits." Mack could then feel confident in asking players to make in-game decisions on their own, but this occurred after Mack had taken time in the dugout to ask players to explain to him why he was doing what he was doing, to teach them through actual game situations, and to test his theories in games rather than in practice to ensure players gained the full perspective of how to survive for nine innings.

In fact, while some of his tactics seemed strange at the time—for example, repositioning players during an inning by waving his scorecard and then later using that motion as a ruse for the opposition—managers to this day continue to use his innovations, even if they don't realize it.

In his first stint as a manager, leading the old Milwaukee Brewers for four seasons, Mack served almost every role for a team—something that's nearly impossible in professional sports today, but something that managers and coaches at other levels could attempt. By learning about others aspects to a baseball team, Mack knew exactly what he was putting on the field for fans to enjoy and the ramifications if a game didn't sell out or if players weren't giving their best efforts.

In his biographical series on Mack, Norman L. Macht wrote this about the man considered the first players' manager: "Do your job, and he left you alone. Need a shot of confidence, and he'd find the right time and the right words. Pull a bonehead play, and he'd call you aside the next day and suggest you try it a different way. He shook off physical errors. … But grouse or complain or talk back to him, and he wouldn't hesitate to snap at you with a barb as sharp as an arrowhead."

Rube Bressler, a pitcher for three seasons for Mack, concurred: "If you made a mistake, Connie never bawled you out on the bench or in front of anybody else. He'd get you alone a few days later, and then say something like, 'Don't you think it would have been better if you'd had made the play this way?'"

Leadership Lessons

On the Diamond: What decisions do you allow your players to make? You can help develop future leaders and future coaches by delegating decisions to players regardless of abilities. How else will they learn to be better players and better men? Compassion and humility go a long way toward giving your team the confidence it needs to play together, to play with enthusiasm, and to play with consistency—all with an eye on winning games. When you empower your players, you also alleviate some of your own stresses, allowing you to focus on the minute details or the big picture as needed rather than micromanaging every aspect of practices and games. If you're a leader of men, you're a leader of the future, so give your players a chance to be leaders.

In the Workplace: What do you do to bring your employees together? How do you help breed future leaders and content yet engaged workers who will perhaps go out into the world and spread their own humane messages? How do you encourage teamwork? You have to allow your emotions to guide you from time to time because you wouldn't have certain reactions if you weren't moved by your feelings. Reconsider your approaches to how you handle your workers on an individual and on a team basis.

Lesson #58: Have Fun—Seriously!
Joe Maddon

"You always want your guys to try hard, but then they get to the point where maybe you're trying to make things happen when you should just let the game play itself out sometimes."

Some managers tend to remain inconspicuous in the dugout, but Joe Maddon isn't such a manager. Known for his Spencer Tracy/Buddy Holly horn-rimmed glasses and his in-your-face personality, Maddon has quickly brought success to the Tampa Bay Rays, winning an American League pennant in 2008 (losing the World Series to the Philadelphia Phillies in five games) and keeping his team above .500 ever since while also earning two Manager of the Year awards. These achievements are no easy feats in the American League East, especially when the competition includes the New York Yankees and the Boston Red Sox.

One way Maddon helps his team relax is, well, to relax the rules. Of course, team rules are generally created by the manager, so on road trips, Maddon allows players to wear whatever they want rather than force them to dress up for each other—and the ensuing cowboy outfits and hockey jerseys and pajamas are a testament to Maddon's casual attitude toward baseball.

"What he tries to do is keep it loose," former Rays catcher Kelly Shoppach said. "There's so many young players there, that they depend on to be impact players, that it's important for those guys to feel comfortable at a young age, virtually as soon as they get there because competing against this division is a challenge. His No. 1 focus is to make sure those guys don't feel like it's a big pressure stage. He brings that into the clubhouse, so we're nice and relaxed all the time and having fun."

Of course, during games, Maddon tends to play the percentages, but he's also not above taking risks if he thinks it will help his club. Early in the 2012 season, with cleanup hitter and first baseman Carlos Pena's batting average nearing the Mendoza line (.200 or worse), Maddon slotted Pena into the leadoff spot. Most managers would have pushed Pena to later in the batting order, but Maddon wanted to test his own theory. Pena responded by going 2-5, collecting three RBIs and a home run in a win against Toronto.

Managers can't teach players how to get out of slumps and bad situations, but they can change certain elements to help players react in new ways.

Leadership Lessons

On the Diamond: It takes little effort to have fun. Just pull back on expectations and allow players to be themselves without being distractions to other players who are trying to do their own thing. But beyond this, try to do some things that will allow fun to grow. Why not take the team bowling or to a miniature golf course or a driving range? This activity will help the players relax in an enjoyable yet someone competitive way and also ensure that not everything the team does is about baseball. Why not see a movie together? Attend a play together? Infuse some culture into your activities, but remember that having fun is key. And in games, you might find that players relax a bit more and take on challenges in new ways without you, as the manager, needing to constantly remind players what to do. Some things are just out of your control, and when you try to control them, you create misery rather than enjoyment, and baseball should be fun, not taxing.

In the Workplace: Never underestimate those team-building exercises that employees engage in outside the office, but don't depend on them alone to create a fun work environment. Relaxing rules and finding opportunities outside the workplace for employees to become involved with the community—and thereby represent their company—will help your workers reenergize themselves and take on difficult situations in better and more successful ways. Taking your staff out to lunch or going to the county fair as a group or taking part in a walk/run event for a charity will show everyone a world outside work, but will also help employees see new ways to tackle problems that might arise. At the same time, you have to allow some issues to work themselves out on their own—as long as those problems aren't festering to such a point that they're impacting everyone's work on a daily basis.

Lesson #59: Never Stop Trying
Charlie Manuel

"I've been in baseball for 40-some years and I haven't been able to figure this game out. That's what makes you stay up late at night. That's what makes you care. That's what makes you come back the next day and try harder. It's hard to explain this game. It's amazing."

For all those detractors who complain about Charlie Manuel's managing style, forget it. He's not going to change because his team is playing poorly. Like many managers, he believes in his methods—honed over time and, if he's still managing, enjoying some success—and finds it easier to make smaller alterations than wholesale modifications. Of course, in a city like Philadelphia, success doesn't always quell naysayers and those calling for your head.

"I think some folks decided to make judgments about me that were based on what they heard," he said, "not on what I did or said. But I'm the same guy. I love comin' to the ballpark every day. Things changed here because of what our team did together—not because of me."

What that team did together was win the National League East from 2007 to 2011 and win two pennants and the 2008 World Series over upstart Tampa Bay. Phillies teams under previous managers struggled to keep pace with the annually dominant Atlanta Braves let alone the other teams in the National League East. And with the Eagles, Flyers, and 76ers offering competitive teams throughout the early part of the 21st century, Philadelphia needed a man like Manuel to return the Phillies to the competitive days the team enjoyed in the late 1970s and early 1980s with Mike Schmidt and Steve Carlton.

"People always want to judge a book by its cover, and that was the case here with Charlie his first few seasons," said Kenneth Shropshire, director of the Sports Business Initiative at the University of Pennsylvania's Wharton School. "The most important thing a management type can do is figure out what he does best and not change from that approach. Charlie looks like he's one of those leaders who says: 'Look, this is who I am, and this is who I'll always be. I'm not changing.'"

But Manuel knows a manager still has to *do* something to help his players.

"You win with good baseball players. But it starts with their character—and we've got great players who love to play baseball. ... And when guys really want to play, they become manageable. They want to get better, and they want to win," he said. "The guys on this team know me and know that I might not say too much, but they understand what is expected. I respect them, but I also know how to make them want to achieve more. ... You get people who want to be in this game, and you're on your way to somethin' good. It's not just me."

Phillies fans hope that "somethin' good" continues for many more years, and Manuel will assuredly be the man to help placate them with wins and championships.

Leadership Lessons

On the Diamond: What gets in your team's way? Parents? Fans? Administrators? Who's trying to push you in certain directions? Who or what is keeping players from developing? How can you help your players improve on yesterday's performance? Last week's performance? How has your team grown from the first day of practice until that last team meeting? What can you carry over to next season and perhaps a different crop of players? Minimize distractions as best as possible and keep everyone working toward figuring the great game of baseball out. It's that endless challenge that will motivate the players who don't let outside influences deter them.

In the Workplace: People haven't solved every issue because they haven't progressed enough as intelligent beings to create enough solutions to suffice all their needs. But they keep trying, and that's what keeps them going every day. Keep trying to find the answers that will make life easier and better for the greatest number of people. In your role as a manager, what are you doing to encourage that atmosphere? Allow inspiration and ideas to flow freely and not be constrained by a suggestion box or weekly meetings. Allow your workers to test their theories to see where they might lead. The day people stop trying is the day they become so complacent that they refuse to believe anything can be better or become better. But they can and they will get better when you encourage your employees to showcase their knowledge and skills despite any perceived odds against them.

Lesson #60: Look Beyond Baseball

Mark Marquess

"These kids are bright and can do so many things, but their focus is to be a major league player. I need to make sure they are getting an education and on track to graduate."

Mark Marquess's coaching resume at Stanford University includes more than 1,400 wins (in the top 10 all time in college baseball), two College World Series titles (1987 and 1988), 15 College World Series regional titles, 25 NCAA tournament appearances, 12 Pac-10 Conference titles, and nine Pac-10 Coach of the Year awards.

In the college game more than at any other level, recruiting players has become the way for baseball teams to stock their rosters with talent. In *The Baseball Coaching Bible*, Coach Marquess explained how important recruiting has become to college baseball:

> In fielding a competitive Division I college baseball team, you must have two ingredients: good players and solid coaching. Early in my coaching career, I thought that coaching was the more critical of these two components. But the longer I have coached, the more convinced I am that recruiting is the lifeblood of a successful college baseball program. You must have talented players if you want to succeed. If I have to hire an assistant baseball coach, the first and most critical factor I consider when making my decision is that coach's ability to recruit. ...

> Obviously, good coaching can and does make a difference, but rarely does superior coaching beat better talent. Recruiting talented players is at least as important to the success of a team as the ability to teach the fundamentals of baseball or manage a baseball game. ...

> In choosing a recruiting philosophy, each college coach must work within a financial budget. I strongly recommend that a coach cut other parts of his budget, whether it be equipment, travel, or other items, to put extra money into his recruiting budget. If sacrifices must be made financially, they should not come at the expense of recruiting. Remember, recruiting is the lifeblood of any successful college athletics program.

Leadership Lessons

On the Diamond: How involved are you in your players' academic affairs? You should try to learn as much as you can about what your players are doing in the classroom. Their performance there might belie their performance on the field, but if they don't keep up with schoolwork, they might not have a chance to take the field. And if they can't take the field, they might continue to lose focus in the classroom and in life, causing a vicious cycle that has ruined too many student-athletes. Nip those problems in the classroom now.

In the Workplace: When times become stressful or overwhelming for your workers, consider bringing in a temporary employee or three to help push projects forward. You'll be doing something good for your employees, for the temps, and for yourself. Short of doing this, perhaps you can move employees into undefined roles for certain processes to gain the best from those people and not have everyone feel like he is under constant pressure to perform.

Lesson #61: Hustle With Muscle

Billy Martin

*"As a manager, I ask only one thing of a player—hustle.
If a player doesn't hustle, it shows the club up and I
show the player up. Hustle is the only thing I really
demand. It doesn't take any ability to hustle."*

During Billy Martin's last season as a Major League player in 1961, someone asked him if he thought about becoming a manager.

"I don't think so because I've got the reputation for being baseball's bad boy and I don't deserve it," he responded. "But I think I'd make a good manager. For one thing, I know how to handle men. That's the secret of managing. For another, I know enough about the game, not fundamentals, but executing. I think I could get the most out of players with common sense and psychology. I'm fiery enough that I'd have their respect. Unfortunately, I don't think I'll ever get the chance and there's nothing in the world that can change that."

But chances he did get, managing the New York Yankees on five different occasions. He also managed the Minnesota Twins, Detroit Tigers, Texas Rangers, and Oakland Athletics, winning four American League division titles and the 1977 World Series with the Yankees.

"The day I become a good loser, I'm quitting baseball," Martin said. "I always had a temper. I think it's nothing to be ashamed of. If you know how to use it, it can help. Temper is something the good Lord gave me and I can't just throw it out the window."

Methods to his madness notwithstanding and opinions about his managing style being as diverse as the ways in which Martin was fired, his achievements speak for themselves. In fact, before Oakland had Moneyball, it had Billyball—a system of play that focused on aggressive baserunning and a scheme enhanced by Rickey Henderson during Martin's three seasons with the Athletics.

"Billy Martin was a man's manager. He treated you like a man, stuck up for you on and off the field, and taught you how to win," former outfielder and 1974 American League MVP Jeff Burroughs said. "He was a little peppery second baseman who didn't have all the natural athletic tools to become a superstar, but he worked hard and learned all the little things about the game to help the team win."

"Billy was the type of guy who just got enraptured with the ball game," said former second baseman Frank Quilici, who played on Martin's 1969 Minnesota Twins team. "He was a very smart baseball man, he was very intense, and he was a perfectionist. That's what he tried to get out of his players."

Leadership Lessons

On the Diamond: Hustle can come in many different forms. It doesn't always mean running. Sometimes, it means making the best decision in a tense situation. You can develop this skill in players who show a lackluster affinity for it through myriad practice situations and exercises, but game errors also lend themselves to teaching hustle tactics, although you'll curse that a bad play occurred in a game. But the idea is to minimize future occurrences, and even if a game situation similar to the one in which the mistake was made never happens again under your watch, you can at least feel confident and content that you fostered a hustling environment.

In the Workplace: Deadlines are often enough pressure for most workers, so when they hear "hustle," their stress levels go up, their work can suffer, and burnout starts to set in. You can prevent these situations by working with your team to simplify processes, finding out who does what best—and is willing to handle such tasks on a constant and/or permanent basis—and offering incentives to your employees when they succeed (and without it seeming like a gimmick to trick your employees into working harder). Knowing your workers' individual strengths and weaknesses regardless of their stated experiences will help them hustle in positive ways and not even feel like they're hustling in haphazard ways let alone putting in more-than-necessary efforts to perhaps achieve minimal goals.

Lesson #62: Challenge Yourself
Mike Martin

*"There's just no game that affects me like baseball.
It's a game that challenges you every single day
just like life. I'm just trying to get home safely."*

When people say "Florida State University," Bobby Bowden logically comes up first. But in Tallahassee, people can't ignore what Mike Martin has done for Seminoles baseball as well as for college baseball. His record speaks for itself: 1,723 wins in 33 seasons (fourth all time in college baseball and third in Division I), five Atlantic Coast Conference titles (FSU joined the ACC in 1992), seven ACC Coach of the Year awards, six Metro Conference Coach of the Year awards, a regional appearance every year, and 15 College World Series appearances—and a title that continues to elude him.

"I don't have to have a national championship to enjoy what I do," said Coach Martin. "I will cherish every moment I have left on the field at Florida State, because I'll be working with young men who want to get better in the sport of baseball. That's what I still get out of it. I'm not going to change. You're doggone right we're going to work to get to Omaha. … And if we get there we darn sure aren't going to go through the motions. But if we don't win it, I'm going to try the next year what I did this year: to get to Omaha and see what happens."

Despite not winning a national title, Coach Martin has earned respect from his fellow coaches.

"Having the trophy is not the true measure of a person's success," said Augie Garrido, who has won five national titles. "It doesn't affect the champion that he is in the minds of all of us that know the truth about this business. We're in the teaching-life-skills business. He's won championships there several hundred times."

Coach Martin doesn't expect to still be coaching when his grandson becomes eligible to play college baseball within the next decade, but he will continue to pursue his dreams—and to help his charges pursue theirs.

"It's the competitiveness … it's so unlike any other sport," he said. "Sometimes, you get 60 games a year where you're competing. That's at least five times more than football and twice as many as basketball. It's exhilarating. You get beat, and you can get over it quick. You win, and you can't enjoy it very long. There's always a game the next day … at least until the last game of the season."

Leadership Lessons

On the Diamond: Wins and championships are great, but when you lose or don't win that league title, you have to look at the individual improvements and goals the team and players made throughout the season. You can give out miniature trophies to every player for something he did well and then present the team with a trophy that encapsulates the season's achievements. And don't think that every award has to be about baseball; don't forget to acknowledge vocal leaders and those who lead by example.

In the Workplace: Giving employees certificates of achievement might seem simple, but it can prove very effective because it gives everyone visual proof that he did something well or that he improved from his last review. And you'll find employees posting these certificates on walls or taking them home to put on fridges.

Lesson #63: Exhibit Your Love
Randy Mazey

*"I think too many people are afraid to show their
emotions when they are passionate about something."*

Randy Mazey had been the head baseball coach for East Carolina University and Charleston Southern University before accepting that position at West Virginia University for the 2013 season—and, he hopes, beyond that. He most recently served as an associate head coach at TCU and has helped develop 14 pitchers who have been drafted in the last five years.

But Coach Mazey has also spent time as a recruitment director (at the University of Tennessee, East Carolina, and the University of Georgia) and knows a thing or two about what will make a good college player—and how that player can make his mark in college baseball:

- *Doing the little things:* "For me, once I recognize that they have the talent to play at this level, I look for the intangibles like hustle, work ethic, how they talk to their teammates and coaches, and how they act when something goes wrong. If I don't like the intangibles, I won't recruit him."

- *Transitioning to college life:* "I'd say the biggest adjustment is that they have just come from being the best player on their high school team to being one of 35 of who were also the best players on their high school team. Now they have to find a new way to separate themselves from the increased level of competition. Also, the fact that they are living on their own for the first time is a huge adjustment period. It takes some time for freshmen to mature off the field, and as hard as we try, there is no way to speed up that process. They have to learn it on their own—it's part of growing up."

- *Separating from the pack:* "They have to find a way to separate themselves from their new competition, so they have to be able to handle it the right way if things do go well at first, which is what happens to every freshman who has ever gone to college. If they have a bad day, which they all will, and have the attitude to learn from it and get better, then they usually find a way to make it into the lineup. If they mope and pout when things go bad, it usually takes those guys a little longer to break into the lineup."

- *Focusing on baseball and being a winner:* "I think the things that stand in the way the most are the distractions. If kids get too caught up in college life, sometimes they tend to lose sight of baseball. The guys who reach their full potential are the guys who are serious about playing this game for a living. A winning ballplayer is a mentality more than anything. Being a winning ballplayer doesn't have anything to do with how good of a player you are, but if you are a good teammate on a winning team, I consider you a winning ballplayer. The great players have a great work ethic and desire to be a great player."

- *Taking it to the next level:* "One thing I would tell young kids who want to play this game for a living is to be a relentless worker at your skill, learn as you go, be a great teammate, respect all of your coaches, and, most importantly, find balance in your life. Don't be obsessed with baseball. People who are obsessed with a particular area of their life are usually really good at the thing they are obsessed with, but every other part of their life suffers. Don't be so caught up in baseball that it has a negative impact on your education or, more importantly, your relationships with people. After all, when baseball is over, the relationships that you have built along the way is what will carry you through the rest of your life."

Leadership Lessons

On the Diamond: When your time as a baseball coach is over, what will you do? When your players' careers end, what will they do? Playing and coaching a sport are but two small yet fleeting moments in someone's life. How can you translate those skills to another field? What other passions do you have? What other dreams do you want to pursue?

In the Workplace: Although the retirement age seems to creep closer and closer to 70 with each passing year, a day will come when you have to move on with life. What will you do? Maybe you can become a mentor or a volunteer, or perhaps you have other goals and dreams. How can you turn your other passions into opportunities to continue to give back to this world?

Lesson #64: Find Opportunities—and Enjoy Them
Joe McCarthy

*"Give a boy a bat and a ball and a place
to play and you'll have a good citizen."*

Opportunities are everywhere in life, and for Joe McCarthy, his opportunity to manage the New York Yankees came at the right time. Not because it was the right time for him, but because it was during the time when the Yankees boasted perhaps its greatest wave of talent. McCarthy managed Babe Ruth and Lou Gehrig at the end of their careers and Joe DiMaggio and Bill Dickey at the beginning of theirs. In McCarthy's 16 seasons in New York, the Yankees won eight pennants and seven World Series, including a then-record four straight from 1936 to 1939.

In 1949, during his second of three seasons as manager of the Boston Red Sox, McCarthy wrote his 10 Commandments for Success in Baseball:

1. Nobody ever became a ballplayer by walking after a ball.
2. You will never become a .300 hitter unless you take the bat off your shoulder.
3. An outfielder who throws in back of a runner is locking the barn after the horse is stolen.
4. Keep your head up and you may not have to keep it down.
5. When you start to slide, slide. He who changes his mind may have to change a good leg for a bad one.
6. Do not alibi on bad hops. Anybody can field the good ones.
7. Always run them out. You never can tell.
8. Do not quit.
9. Do not fight too much with the umpires. You cannot expect them to be as perfect as you are.
10. A pitcher who hasn't control hasn't anything.

"He was the best manager I ever saw," said Boston's Hall of Fame outfielder Ted Williams. "McCarthy was always on top of the game and knew the limits and abilities of his players."

Leadership Lessons

On the Diamond: One great way to see what your players can do is to put them at different positions in a practice game. Each inning, move everyone to a new position, allowing everyone to play every position in a nine-inning game. Maybe no one will acquit himself like Jose Oquendo and show an ability to play every position with some success, but you'll learn a lot about a player's abilities and strengths and weaknesses. If you have enough of these intrasquad games, you can also allow every player to bat from a different spot in the batting order, thereby seeing how he might react to different situations based on what happens before he bats. One day, managers and coaches will stop batting pitchers in the nine hole and create lineups that spread the hitting talent throughout a lineup rather than batting the best hitters right away. After the first inning, seldom will the 1-2-3 batters lead off an inning again. Keep this in mind as you watch your players perform in these practice games.

In the Workplace: Most employees know their limitations and their talents, but if you think you can pull this off without much difficulty—and without too much consternation and disruption—you might take a day to put your workers in different positions and have them perform new tasks as well as possibly learn new skills. This might prove too difficult to attempt, but how much can it hurt to try for a day? Workers might learn something new about themselves, and you should gain some new insights about your employees. This will also help each employee see what issues his coworkers have to handle on a daily basis, thereby hopefully increasing their admiration and respect for each other.

Lesson #65: Accommodate Your Players' Needs
John McGraw

"Learn to know every man under you, get under his skin, know his faults. Then cater to him—with kindness or roughness as his case may demand."

John McGraw knew a lot about roughness, but he also knew a lot about how to manage baseball players. In his 31 years as the skipper for the New York Giants, his teams won 10 National League pennants and three World Series. In fact, his 2,763 wins still rank second all time, and he continues to hold the National League record for most wins with 2,669.

Although part of Ned Hanlon's coaching tree with the old Baltimore Orioles, McGraw weaned himself into his own kind of manager and developed a list he called McGraw's Bible, as presented in Leonard Koppett's *The Man in the Dugout*:

1. Tactics to gain a small edge—bunting, a hit-and-run play, cutoff throws—could be developed further than they had, and could make a big difference to winning and losing if refined "scientifically."
2. Personal discipline and physical conditioning were essential to season-long effectiveness.
3. The manager's authority had to be accepted as absolute, not only in game play decisions but in practice and off-field self-care, to make better tactics work.
4. Aggressiveness was a primary asset.
5. Speed—of foot and brain—helped you win.
6. Deciding where and when a man should play was as important as recognizing his generalized abilities.
7. It's us against them.

In time, McGraw would refine these concepts and assert himself more with his teams. He would have an enduring impact on many a man by sticking to his principles.

"I worked for McGraw for only one year, but I learned more that season than in all the years before—or since," said Hall of Fame pitcher Burleigh Grimes. "The science of pitching took on a new meaning. 'Burleigh,' he told me, 'don't let them hit behind the runner all the time,' and he showed me how to use my curve to get righthanded batters to pull the ball to the left side. Balls hit to the left side with men on base meant more double plays and fewer runners advancing from first to third on singles, and that meant fewer runs for them, which meant more victories and more money for me. I ended up winning 270 games in my career, but if I'd known earlier what McGraw taught me, I could've won 300. He was the smartest man I ever played for."

Leadership Lessons

On the Diamond: Early in spring training, tell players that they're going to play a nine-inning game and that everyone should pay attention to what each other is doing. Afterward, pair up players and have them write assessments of each other. Use these as extra information about how to handle problems players show you throughout that game and in future practices. Then, you can furnish them with the needed training and tools to overcome those issues. When you rely on your players for help with assessment, you're helping them take responsibility for each other.

In the Workplace: Workers don't often have time or the desire to practice certain techniques. But if you can find ways to incorporate training into regular tasks, then you can quickly assess how well someone does a task and what he might need to further increase his success rate. This could be something as simple as having an employee extend his knowledge about a computer program to take on a new task. If he has as aptitude with, say, creating charts in Excel, then he can surely learn how to present those charts in another program, such as PowerPoint.

Lesson #66: Focus on Today
Bill McKechnie

"You can't even celebrate a victory. If you win today, you must start worrying about tomorrow. If you win a pennant, you start worrying about the World Series. As soon as that's over, you start worrying about the next season."

Some managers never have a chance to manage a team in the World Series, but McKechnie not only took three different teams to the World Series—a feat later accomplished by Dick Williams—but he also won two titles and revitalized two iconic National League franchises: the Pittsburgh Pirates and the Cincinnati Reds.

Although his 1925 Pirates had great hitters, his 1940 Reds had great pitchers, including Bucky Walters, Paul Derringer, and Johnny Vander Meer, who had thrown consecutive no-hitters in 1938, McKechnie's first year with the Reds. McKechnie had concise attitudes about how his pitchers should approach their craft:

- Pitchers couldn't rely solely on a fastball. They also needed to develop a curve that could be thrown for strikes (rather than, say, trying to get the hitter to swing and miss).
- Pitchers couldn't throw sliders. He thought the pitch hurt arms and shortened careers.
- Pitchers needed to build confidence and believe in their pitches—and have faith in their ability to win games.
- Pitchers should try to complete games. This meant developing the endurance to last nine innings—and beyond if necessary.
- Pitchers must refrain from getting angry and should remain focused on their pitching tasks.

Because his pitchers knew McKechnie would yank them from a game if they didn't comply with his rules, they adjusted to his maxim of "Don't get mad; stay focused and give the next pitch your best shot."

"McKechnie knew the capabilities of his bullpen better than any manager I ever saw," said Hall of Fame manager Al Lopez, who played under McKechnie with the Boston Bees (now the Atlanta Braves). "He knew his relievers so well that he always had the right man ready for the right spot. And the man's arm was always fresh and strong. Bill also had amazing patience. 'A hasty decision,' he used to say, 'is usually a mistake.'"

Leadership Lessons

On the Diamond: Mistakes will happen. They're inevitable. How you and your team react to them, though, can make all the difference between having a good team and a great team. But when they occur, focus on them today and then let them go. This isn't to say you shouldn't deal with them in practice or even try to make a quick adjustment during a game. But you can't erase something that has happened. All you can do is work through it—and take time in practice to help your team learn how to handle it better the next time it occurs in a game. This approach will prepare players to not become unwound when mistakes happen again—and they *will* happen.

In the Workplace: How do you handle employee errors? What are the ramifications? Consider having practice sessions in which you discuss error-riddled situations and go through the motions of determining where the mistake occurred and how to rectify it. You might also find flaws in processes, thus opening up opportunities for employees to prove themselves and showcase their skills in meeting and thwarting challenges. Asking your workers to tell you how an error happened will help them much better than your yelling at them for the error. You can't fix problems through yelling or through not trying to understand why something happened.

Lesson #67: Never Let Age Define You
Jack McKeon

"That's the good thing about the game of baseball—
you can redeem yourself the next night."

Jack McKeon proved that it's never too late to achieve great success in baseball. In 2003, after the Florida Marlins started 16-22, the team hired the 72-year-old McKeon to manage the team. They had no easy road that season, but they finished a respectable 91-71 and won the National League wild card. The Marlins then proceeded to beat the San Francisco Giants in the National League Division Series, the Chicago Cubs in the National League Championship Series, and the New York Yankees in the World Series, winning its second championship in the franchise's very short existence.

Although the Marlins couldn't retain its star players and remain consistent winners in the National League East, McKeon left an impact on that 2003 Marlins team—an impression extracted from his many years in professional baseball as a catcher, general manager, and Minor and Major League manager. Don't be surprised, though, if even at age 82 or beyond that he gains another opportunity to manage a baseball team.

McKeon listed some keys to staying young and enjoying life:
- Enjoy each game, each pitch, nothing is promised.
- You are never too old to become older and never too old to become younger.
- Draw lessons from the past, don't live in the past.
- Steer clear of too much self-examination; you don't want the small stuff to make you sweat.
- Speak plainly and carry a big stogie.
- If effort lags, light 'em up. Players need and want discipline.
- Play your hunches.
- Failure isn't fatal.
- Have a role for your role players.
- When a player stumbles, help him up.
- The Good Lord has a plan for you.
- Get to the ballpark early.
- Never complain when your wife goes shopping.
- Always pack an extra box of cigars.

Leadership Lessons

On the Diamond: Keep in mind that "the next night" is also a metaphor for the next week or the next season or the next opportunity. You never know when you might have a chance to rectify a bad decision. Sometimes, you have to create that chance for yourself because no one knows better than you what you need to do. As a leader for your team, you're in a unique position to gauge talent and cull prior experiences to help your team combine these elements to work through poor choices and disappointing losses. You can't change the past, but you can change how you react to it, and as a coach, you should try to instill this concept in your players. Then, when something bad happens again, they can quickly readjust and focus on the next play rather than worrying about what just happened, which can be addressed at a later time.

In the Workplace: When your workers don't come through on time or with success, what consequences do they suffer? Better yet, how do you help them redeem themselves? What kind of timeline do you give people to show you they *do* know what they're doing? Don't forget how you handled situations when you were in their shoes, and use that experience and expertise to guide your employees toward a redemption process. Use these moments as teaching opportunities, not times to berate your employees. You build confidence through allowing people to work through their struggles, but you can't neglect helping them find the tools they need to do that.

Lesson #68: Take Chances
Pat Moran

"The breaks are everything in this game, but you can't count on them one way or the other. Now you get them, and now the other fellow has his innings. You can't alibi anything on the breaks. When you lose a game forget it and start out hustling for the next. That has always been my policy. No pennant predictions. No looking ahead; no counting any chickens in the egg, but just hustling all the time, and playing every game for all there is in it."

Pat Moran might still remain unknown to most baseball fans if not for the infamous 1919 World Series between his Cincinnati Reds and William "Kid" Gleason's Chicago White Sox. Although Moran had led the Philadelphia Phillies in his first season to its first pennant in 1915 since its 1883 inception, once World War I started in 1918, the Phillies felt the impact, falling to below .500, causing the team to fire Moran. In Cincinnati, Christy Mathewson left his manager post during the 1918 season to join the U.S. Army, during which time he contracted tuberculosis, so the Reds hired Moran for the 1919 season. And as they say, the rest is history, as the 1919 World Series story has been told countless other times in countless other ways.

Cincinnati hadn't finished in first place since its first season in the American Association—the precursor league to the National League—in 1882. But Moran changed the team's entire atmosphere and not only led the team to its first pennant in franchise history, but also to its first World Series title. Two areas that Reds team focused on were defense and the details: pickoffs, cutoffs, fielding bunts, backing up teammates, double steals, and the hit-and-run play.

"Moran is a quiet, serious fellow. He never 'rides' his players. He never finds fault with anything except for the purpose of explaining a mistake and making sure that it won't be repeated," Robert Edgren wrote in a 1919 newspaper article about Moran. "The interests of his men were his interests. He looked out for them just as an army officer must look out for the men under him to make his command efficient to the limit."

Cincinnati's best assets in 1919 were its pitchers. Moran had spent most of his playing career as a catcher in Boston, Chicago, and Philadelphia, thus preparing him to handle his star pitchers on his 1919 staff. Two techniques Moran used with his pitchers were to stand behind the catcher when the pitcher warmed up before a game, telling him to imagine himself in certain situations, and to have catchers offer several signs rather than the customary single pitch signal. No wonder Rod Eller, Dutch Ruether, and Slim Sallee had career years in 1919.

"It was Pat who made a pitcher out of me and I was fortunate to play under him in both Philadelphia and Cincinnati," Hall of Fame pitcher Eppa Rixey said. "Few men that I've ever known in baseball knew the fine arts of pitching as did Moran."

"As leader, it is my business to give orders, and these are always carried out. Not by the 'mailed fist' method, as I do not believe in that style, but as one friend to another. The players carry them out because they have confidence in me," said Moran.

Leadership Lessons

On the Diamond: One of baseball's greatest facets is that the defense controls the ball, which occurs in no other sport. More often than not, good defense can shut down good offense, but a good offense can also find ways to take advantage of a good defense. You have to make the most of your opportunities, which is three outs an inning and 27 for a game. Sometimes, things won't go your team's way; other times, they certainly will. But you can't do much more than prepare rudimentary plans for them and hope your players take advantage—whether hitting or fielding or pitching. Some days, factors you can't even begin to imagine will play a part in a victory or in a loss. Let those factors go after a game because next time, those factors might change the entire game in a different way. Revel in the achievements, and then let go; grimace about the errors, and then let go—you'll be deep in another ball game before you know it.

In the Workplace: Don't worry about your competition too much. If you can have your employees focus on their tasks and their goals, then achievements and success will come. When you spend time plotting how to respond to the competition's success, then you lose sight of well-honed processes and become less effective in meeting demands. Be proactive in doing what you do best as individuals and as a team.

Lesson #69: Prepare to Succeed
Jim Morris

*"I admire what our players do. The level of competition
these players play at is very tough because we are
expected to be the top team in the country. Our guys
are also competing at a level academically at one of
the top institutions and are pretty good at staying
out of trouble. They know what's right and wrong."*

During Jim Morris's time at the University of Miami, no other program in the country has earned more trips to the College World Series than the Hurricanes. In more than 30 years as a head coach and with almost 1,400 career wins at the collegiate level, Coach Morris knows solid plans can lead to solid success.

In an article for JUGS Sports, Coach Morris laid out how he readies his team:

I have always prided myself in attempting to prepare my team for every situation. If anything happens in a game and I have not practiced and covered that situation then I better figure out how to incorporate it into my practice plan. I also believe that we must attempt to ultimately try to practice at game speed.

One thing we do is put the JUGS machine on the mound with a pitcher and defense behind the machine. I then want to practice with the machine throwing with the following situations with 0, 1 and 2 outs:

1. No one on base
2. Man on 1st
3. Man on 2nd
4. Man on 1st and 2nd
5. Man on 3rd
6. Man on 2nd and 3rd
7. Bases loaded

With this controlled situation you can explain to the players offensively and defensively what you expect and how to handle the situation.

I want our players to be able to 'play the game' offensively and defensively. Repetition and drills make it happen.

Leadership Lessons

On the Diamond: Even at the professional level—but especially at the college, high school, and Little League levels—players have more going on in their lives than baseball. While their levels of passion and commitment might differ at each level—and professional athletes *do* need to be motivated sometimes—they're still human beings who have other goals in life. You have to keep that in mind when working with your players. Specifically, design your drills so they're very focused and don't incorporate too many extra elements. For example, when practicing pickoff moves, stick to having one base runner to start, helping your catcher, pitcher, and infielders focus on this most common situation. Once they understand the dynamics involved—and have practiced with extremely fast runners and even somewhat indifferent runners who might try to steal now and again—then you can add more runners. Your players should take this same approach with their other goals, especially their academic ones.

In the Workplace: Your employees have more going on in their lives than just their jobs. Keep this in mind when delegating tasks, although you should try to treat everyone fairly and equally. You eventually learn who has family demands or other goals they're pursuing on their own time, and this will help you when you assign responsibilities—although the "help" comes in the form of not overloading some people and not underappreciating others based on this knowledge. This approach will prevent resentment from developing and will help breed a content workforce.

Lesson #70: Find Your Niche
Danny Murtaugh

*"The more patient you are, the better manager you'll be.
When I first came up as manager I was too demanding.
I had to learn never to expect a man to do something he
is not capable of doing. Now I try to analyze and find out
their capabilities and then never ask them to exceed them."*

For all his success in Pittsburgh as a manager, including World Series titles in 1960 (when Bill Mazeroski hit a home run in the bottom of the ninth inning in Game 7 to defeat the New York Yankees) and 1971 (when Roberto Clemente became the first Latino to win the World Series MVP), Danny Murtaugh might have made the most history on September 1, 1971. For a game against the cross-state Philadelphia Phillies, Murtaugh filled out a lineup complete with minorities—a first in Major League history.

"When it comes to making out the lineup, I'm color blind and my athletes know it. They don't know it because I told them, but they know it because they are familiar with the way I operate," Murtaugh said.

"It was a good thing to hear what Danny Murtaugh said after the game, and there's no doubt in my mind that he meant that," said all-star first baseman Al Oliver. "He could play hunches as well as any manager that I played for. He might start a guy that hadn't played in two or three weeks. He may have had a hunch that a guy may do well against a certain pitcher. Whether it was a hunch that night or whatever you want to call it, it was baseball history."

Murtaugh clearly had a sense about what his players could achieve and seldom hesitated to allow them to do it.

"If I were a manager, Danny Murtaugh is the kind of manager I'd want to be like," said Hall of Famer Willie Stargell. "He doesn't demand respect; he commands it. He knows how to handle players, to get the most out of them. He doesn't say much, but when he does, you listen because you know it means something."

Leadership Lessons

On the Diamond: You'll never know what your players are capable of—and what their limits might be—unless you give them a chance to show you what they can do. And even if you notice their weaknesses, that's no guarantee they can't come through in that area in time. Running through drills isn't enough to assess player ability. You have to allow them to play simulation games, and you have to track their performances in actual games. In Zane Grey's novel *The Young Pitcher*, Coach Worry Arthurs has Ken Ward, one of his players, throw batting practice during the team's first session together. Throughout the beginning of the novel, Ken tries to find his place on the team and fails in all regards, although he becomes much better at hitting, which gives him the confidence he needs to ask his coach if he'll let him try pitching. And pitch he does. Give your players a chance to voice their opinions about what they'd like to do—and then see if they can do it to your satisfaction.

In the Workplace: Patience can be an incredibly hard skill to learn in fast-paced environments, and although you try to vet your hires to ensure they have the abilities you need them to have to perform the tasks you need completed, some people have skills they've not been allowed to pursue for one reason or another. If you're new to a company or have a new employee, take the time to converse with your employees to allow them the chance to let you know what they can do and what they'd like to learn to do. Companies should encourage this more rather than keep employees stuck in their stagnant roles.

Lesson #71: Make Today Memorable

Johnny Oates

"If we have 14 months or two years, why waste a day?
We spend so much time in our lives taking care of
the baggage of our past, or worrying about
the future, we forget to live today."

Before Johnny Oates died from a brain tumor in 2004, he had started to help put the Texas Rangers firmly on the baseball map. He would assuredly express his pride that the Rangers have continued to enjoy success in recent years, and those teams can thank Oates for his efforts in helping them—even if in spirit.

In Oates' seven seasons in Texas, he led the Rangers to three American League West titles, and although these teams didn't progress to the World Series, they did have a leader who preached focusing on what players can do today to achieve their goals.

"Really there's only one day of the week that has any importance, and that's today," he said. "You can't do anything about yesterday and you can't do anything about tomorrow. It's just today."

A former catcher who played for legendary managers Earl Weaver, Danny Ozark, Tommy Lasorda, and Dick Howser, Oates learned how to manage games and players—a trait that comes in handy for almost any good manager or coach.

"He was the perfect catcher for me," said Hall of Fame pitcher Jim Palmer, who went 10-0 for the Baltimore Orioles in 1972 with Oates catching him. "He was smart, always full of questions. He knew what he could do and what he couldn't. He worked so hard all the time. You have a lot of respect for somebody like that."

"Johnny handled adversity as well as anybody I've ever seen," said Tom Schieffer, former Rangers president. "During losing streaks he was at his steadiest. He never ducked out. He had everybody's respect."

Perhaps one of his successors as manager for the Rangers summed up best what kind of man Johnny Oates was: "He's the most ethical, moral man I've ever been around," said Buck Showalter.

Leadership Lessons

On the Diamond: What are you doing today for those you love and for the world around you? Pretend your local airport has lost your emotional baggage and all the burdens you carry with you throughout a day. Impress upon your players how important today is, and help them focus on getting better in the now rather than worrying about tomorrow.

In the Workplace: Leave your personal problems at home, but don't forget to help employees who might have struggles outside work. Join together as a group to work through problems. Remember, today is a blessing and that no better time exists to make the world a better place. Focus on how what you do as individuals and as a team can help with that endeavor. Regardless of your field, you can find ways to make a difference.

Lesson #72: Create New Paths to Success

Dan O'Brien

*"The great players grind it out the same way every day
regardless of outcome. They play the same if they're
up by 10, down by 10, in a slump or on fire."*

Dan O'Brien is the current head baseball coach at Santa Clara University, where he took over in 2012 after coaching for 14 years at the University of California at San Diego in Division II. In his time with the Tritons, he became the winningest coach in school history and won National Coach of the Year honors twice. His teams also won four conference tournaments and made two NCAA national championship finals.

Coach O'Brien detailed some thoughts about what he looks for in college players:

- *Standing out:* "There are a lot of solid ballplayers out there with a lot of ability. We're looking for the guy that comes early, stays late, loves to be in the clutch situations and can't wait to come through for his teammates, and pick them up on and off the field whenever he can. Get a group of guys like that together and you can accomplish anything!"

- *Making the transition from high school:* "He needs to understand that high school baseball is relatively easy, and that a lack of preparation prior to getting to the next level will hit you like a ton of bricks when you arrive. Most of our freshmen think they've been working hard when in reality they don't understand how hard you need to work to get ready. Once they arrive, they also need to learn to slow the game down. That takes time, but the game will be much faster."

- *Preparing to play:* "What's going on between their ears. If everyone agrees that the game is 90% mental, then why don't players and coaches spend more time on the mental game? The mental game, in my mind, is without question the difference maker for players, coaches and programs."

- *Becoming a winner:* "[They] can take a punch, and then another, and then another, and then make a play. The ability to handle adversity is the key to success. The game is about being consistent."

- *Taking it to the next level:* "Desire. If you want it bad enough you will grind your way to success. It's also important to find the right fit. You can grind it out all you want at the best program in the country and you may still get cut. Find a fit and grind."

Leadership Lessons

On the Diamond: What can you do to increase success in the mental game? Sometimes, specific baseball actions become their own detriment. For example, fielding grounders for an hour or hitting 100 pitches can develop skills, but they can also become overkill. Try to engage your players in activities that relate to those areas they need to continue to strengthen, but use other means to help them. For example, have them field footballs or hit eggs or small tomatoes or try to catch plastic bottles. The actions are the same—generally speaking—if not perhaps a little more messy, but they will help players focus on fundamentals and details by reframing tactics.

In the Workplace: If workers seem to struggle to handle certain tasks or have become somewhat bored or complacent with responsibilities they once did without breaking a sweat—and without making errors—then try some new ways to accomplish old tasks. This approach will differ from setting to setting, but try having workers start fresh with a process. For example, have them reconsider their first step when getting an assignment. Is that really the best first step? Can something be done differently that might make the task more pleasurable on some level?

Lesson #73: Build Familial Relationships
Danny Ozark

*"Contrary to popular belief, I have always
had a wonderful repertoire with my players."*

Some managers seem destined to just help a team stop the bleeding during a stretch of bad seasons. Danny Ozark might seem like such a manager, seeing as his players considered him too easygoing. But for three seasons in the 1970s, he helped turn around a franchise and prepared it for glory yet to come—and glory almost not realized.

From its inception as the Philadelphia Quakers in 1883 through the 1979 season, the Philadelphia Phillies had struggled mightily as a franchise. Despite National League pennants in 1915 and 1950 (with the Whiz Kids), the Phillies still couldn't win a World Series. Before that changed in 1980 under manager Dallas Green, Ozark and the Phillies won the American League East from 1976 to 1978 but lost the NLCS every season.

And despite his penchant for malapropisms, Ozark learned from his managing experience at the Minor League level that he needed to have great *rapport* with his players.

"He was a good friend, my first major league manager and played a major role in the early years of my career, and was instrumental in building us into prominence in the mid-1970s," said Hall of Fame third baseman Mike Schmidt. "He brought a wealth of baseball experience from his years with the [Brooklyn/Los Angeles] Dodgers to Philadelphia, and we were fortunate to have him as our leader throughout that time."

"That's the way Danny was," said Ginny Ozark, his wife of 60 years. "He used to call me from the ballpark and say, 'I'm bringing a couple of kids home.' I'd say, 'How many?' All of a sudden from five to 20 players, he'd bring the whole ball club. He took care of them like he was their father."

Leadership Lessons

On the Diamond: Players often spend more time with their coaches than their families. This is all the more reason to find ways to help your team feel like a family: Go on a picnic, build a float for a parade, enter a charity walk, rent a cabin for a weekend, or just spend time engaged in any activity not called baseball. You'll be surprised what you learn about your players—and yourself.

In the Workplace: Workers tend to bemoan retreats and training sessions. Why not find ways to connect with each other and with the community by volunteering at schools or joining a bowling league or having someone host a potluck dinner once a month? Sometimes, when workers aren't stuck in an office or their usual confines, they'll open up a lot more. And when you get to know your employees better, you become a more efficient manager.

Lesson #74: Improve Your Dedication
Jim Penders

*"You're either getting better or
worse every second of the day."*

As an up-and-coming college baseball coach who has won Big East Coach of the Year awards in 2006, 2010, and 2011 at the University of Connecticut—and as a coach with a rich pedigree, as his father, brother, grandfather, and uncle (basketball coach Tom Penders) have all coached amateur teams—Jim Penders understands the challenges players have on collegiate teams.

Specifically, Coach Penders knows it's no easy transition for freshmen who have left behind star status with their high school teams.

"For some freshmen, it's failing for the first time. Most of them struggle with distractions and focusing now that Mom or Dad is not telling them, 'Hey it's time to do your hitting lessons.' They may have been perceived as hard workers in the past, but now they get to choose how hard they work. They have to figure out how to do it on their own—not just on the baseball field, but in the classroom and when they're studying," he said. "Even socially, they have to decide what are the best choices for them on Thursday night; will they be the last guy to leave the party or the first guy?"

Coach Penders' 2011 team earned a trip to Super Regionals and had 10 players drafted by major league teams. He offered a keen insight about what helped those players succeed.

"A winning player is one who takes his work and preparation extremely seriously, but not himself too seriously. That's a winner. If a guy can be described as a great teammate, that's a winning guy. And not just on the field, but in life," he said. "These kind of guys have the best chance of being the most successful and effective human beings."

Selflessness has become an unusual characteristic for baseball players in recent times, but when a teammate worries more about the team than his individual stats, then the team can not only enjoy more success but also potentially achieve its season-long goals.

"Obviously, you have to have a certain level of talent; however, the guys that are willing to play hurt or give that extra effort when they're tired, those are the ones that separate themselves," Coach Penders said. "The guys that are doing something to get better on the field, in the classroom, and socially every day are the guys that are going to be successful."

Leadership Lessons

On the Diamond: You assume everyone on the team loves baseball. But that's not the point. Are they giving their best efforts and being good teammates? If not, address that by acknowledging players who play when hurt or who did something unselfish to help the team. Those who love the game will show it in how they react to such a speech. That doesn't mean you cut them from the team. But it means you take the time to find out what they care about. Then, once you have that knowledge, you can decide what's best for them and the team—letting the players make the decisions about what happens next.

In the Workplace: It's a positive attitude to believe that everyone is giving his best, but that's not always true. Some people do what they can to get by. You'll notice. And then you'll need to act to circumvent problems. You can't change people any more than you can force them to do something they don't want to do. But you can encourage them by showing them what other people are doing. Don't let someone's perceived pride force your team into difficult situations. Be a good manager, and try to help struggling workers make great strides.

Lesson #75: Manage by Results
Lou Piniella

"Don't let names fool you. Production wins."

In his 23 seasons as a major league manager—including leading the 1990 Cincinnati Reds to their last World Series title—Piniella culled some significant philosophies for how to manage:

- *On risks:* "Tactically, I like to take chances. I like an aggressive style of game. If we're hitting the ball well, I don't believe in us running ourselves out of innings. I want to give these guys a full opportunity to make three outs with the bat. If we're not scoring runs, and we're struggling somewhat, then we can do a little bit of squeezing, a little more hit and running, those sort of things, optional steals. I let these guys play. I recognize fully as a manager, the players win and lose baseball games on the field."

- *On sabermetrics:* "If I had to go gut or numbers, I like numbers. I like percentages. I believe fully that this is a percentage game, and the more I keep percentages on our side, the better chance we have to win as a team. And I know that at times you have to go against the grain a little bit to keep everybody honest. ... Numbers don't lie. I use [numbers] to rest people, I use them for spot starts, I use them to bring a relief pitcher into the game. If I see that we're playing a team that two of my relievers pitched well against, I'll rest them for that series and try to get away with keeping them nice and fresh. ... If a particular pitcher struggles against a team and I can juggle to give him a start against another team, we do that. So we do everything that we can to keep the numbers on our side."

- *On adjustments:* "I have the advantage of sitting here and seeing how every hitter attacks or adjusts or takes every pitch. I was a hitter up here for 17 and a half years, so I have a pretty good idea of how hitters think and don't think. Some of them don't think, they just swing. And then we have some definite ideas of how to pitch different hitters if they're hitting in the .250 range, if they're hitting in the .280 range, if they're hitting .315 or .320. There's a reason why some guys are hitting .315 and others are hitting .280. Whatever it is, you can't pitch them the same."

Leadership Lessons

On the Diamond: Don't let names on the backs of the jerseys undermine you. Last week's results might not happen in this week's game, or the last game's hero might become today's goat. Do what feels right in any given situation and by using whatever barometer you feel comfortable with. You're the coach. You don't have to answer to your players. They need to play for the name on the front of the jersey. This is their chance to leave a mark on their program—and it can be a solid and memorable mark or a jagged and miserable one.

In the Workplace: Sometimes, you just have to stand back and see what people accomplish and evaluate them on that rather than on who they are. Don't let arbitrary designations—tenure, child of a community leader, or where someone went to school—prevent you from requiring strong results from workers. Maybe you're a numbers-driven manager or you prefer to assess employees through other means. But be consistent—in how you appraise workers and in how you confront those who aren't pulling their weight.

Lesson #76: Compliment Your Complements
Ron Polk

*"Success as a coach should never be
defined solely by the scoreboard!"*

Ron Polk isn't known as the Father of Southeastern Conference Baseball for nothing. His Mississippi State teams won five Southeastern Conference championships, and Polk led squads to 23 NCAA tournaments appearances and eight College World Series. Despite retiring in 2008, his 1,373 career wins still rank him in the top 10 all time.

In *The Baseball Coaching Bible*, Coach Polk described how imperative it is to hire a diligent coaching staff and have strong support personnel:

> Probably no task is more important in organizing and orchestrating a winning program than surrounding oneself with quality assistant coaches, managers, trainers, secretaries, a sports information coordinator, and even bat girls. It is vital that all support personnel work toward goals each day to produce positive results both on and off the baseball field.
>
> Each year I produced for coaches and support personnel detailed job descriptions and administrative responsibility sheets. Everyone fully understood what I expected of them and how their jobs would enable us to meet the daily obligations of the baseball program. We held daily meetings with the entire coaching staff and scheduled periodic meetings with the other personnel to ensure everyone had a way to share information with the baseball program. …
>
> Securing dedicated, first-class individuals to work with student-athletes and the public is crucial to the success of any program. I believe that to have a successful coaching career you must surround yourself with quality people. You must encourage both positive and negative comments from these associates to ensure that you meet all the needs of the baseball program. …
>
> Those working within a quality baseball program will quickly understand that a major investment of time is required from all involved. To do even the little things takes a time commitment. This investment of time in doing a first-class job will reap major benefits in the results achieved by the program, not only in wins on the field but also in public relations. Further, the student-athletes will respect the program and learn that careful preparation will be useful in later life.

Leadership Lessons

On the Diamond: You can't do everything on your own. Surround yourself with quality people who can help you with all your team's goals, freeing you up for those areas you're most knowledgeable and passionate about and preventing you from burning out too early in your career. But don't forget to let those people know how you feel about them. If they're quality people, they'll reciprocate those feelings.

In the Workplace: Almost every business has someone who does those little tasks that actually keep a lot of processes running smoothly. If you have a role in hiring these people, you'll quickly know what these people can offer you and your team. Take advantage of their talents and let them know how much you appreciate their work. They'll surely return that respect in kind.

Lesson #77: Resist Urges to Quit
Gary Pullins

"The will to win ... must be stronger than the fear of defeat."

In his 28 years as a college baseball coach, Gary Pullins won more than 1,000 games and led Brigham Young University to seven Western Athletic Conference titles. He also earned coaching awards on the conference, division, and regional levels.

In *The Baseball Coaching Bible* (in a chapter he coauthored with legendary pitching coach Tom House), Coach Pullins presented training regimens that good coaches have taught for more than a century—techniques that sports science has shown are biomechanically sound:

- *Mental conditioning:* "Mental conditioning is really both mental and emotional management, an absolute that starts with persistence. Baseball is a game of failure. If a youngster cannot deal with striking out, making errors, giving up hits, and losing, he'll never succeed in the game. Good coaches intuitively teach (1) managing feelings of failure, (2) not following the path of failure, (3) visualizing success in the face of failure, and (4) affirming the process of success. Persistence is reinforced when a player can identify why he did or didn't do the job and then is given the means by which to maintain good, or avoid bad, performances."

- *Physical conditioning:* "We do physical conditioning to develop baseball strength, not body-building, wide-body, which-way-to-the-beach strength. Throwing and hitting require functional strength and endurance specific to those movements. ... Strength is built with resistance training; endurance is built with a combination of light-resistance, large-repetition resistance training, plus actual throwing and swinging. Both strength and endurance training must be specific to the positions and movements of baseball."

- *Nutritional conditioning:* "Nutrition is blood chemistry. Blood chemistry is weight management; wound healing; recovery times; aerobic and anaerobic efficiency; fuel for nerves, muscle, and connective tissue; bone to prepare, compete, and repair. To maximize the benefits of nutrition, think food—combining it, rotating it, supplementing it, enhancing it."

- *Biomechanical conditioning:* This relates to developing a dynamic balance, a stable posture, forearm-elbow integrity at foot strike, an axis of torso rotation relative to stride length (75 percent for pitchers and 50 percent for hitters), and forearm-elbow integrity at release point or contact.

Leadership Lessons

On the Diamond: While it's not necessarily your responsibility to ensure your players are in good mental and physical condition, you can still find ways to include conditioning aspects in your program. Bring in a dietician or nutritionist or a physical therapist or a sports science expert to talk with your players about how good physical and mental traits will allow them to pinpoint their own weaknesses and work on them. Likewise, a healthy player should equate to a healthy student—whether in the classroom or in life.

In the Workplace: Businesses don't take enough time to ensure the health and mental well-being of their employees, but it takes little effort and little time to have a health specialist or even a psychologist come to the workplace to discuss ways employees can ensure they're taking care of themselves and giving the best they can to their employer. As a manager, you should work with other managers to bring such a program to fruition.

Lesson #78: Speak With Authority
Frank Robinson

"I had no trouble communicating.
The players just didn't like what I had to say."

Frank Robinson could be, well, frank with his players. As a player, he let his bat speak for himself, finishing his Hall of Fame career with almost 3,000 hits and nearly 600 home runs. As a manager, he had to take a different approach: Make the best decision for this situation, and then live with it.

In fact, that's what he did in 1975 when he accepted the Cleveland Indians' offer to be their manager. Not only did he also play outfield during his two full seasons helming the Indians, but he became the first black manager in Major League history. He had wanted to manage after his career, not during, but to further the cause for minorities in baseball, he knew he needed to take advantage of the opportunity while it was there.

He managed the Indians for a short time before taking over the San Francisco Giants in the early 1980s and the Montreal Expos and the Washington Nationals in the early 2000s. But squeezed in between, he managed a struggling Baltimore Orioles team that went 54-107 (the Orioles fired Cal Ripken Sr. after the team lost its first six games) in 1988 and then finished 87-75 in 1989, earning Manager of the Year honors for Robinson.

"I do some things off the wall. I do things by instinct, by gut feeling, about what I see out there. It's a little odd to some people, especially today, with such hands-on ownership groups and the advice they're getting from other people. You're rubbing people the wrong way. I know that it could be used against me, and I know that some people have used that stuff today in selecting front office people and managers," Robinson said. "They feel like today's management and people in baseball have to be computer-savvy and numbers-savvy. But I've always said—and I'm not disrespecting numbers—that I don't manage that way. I manage by instincts, what I see."

Leadership Lessons

On the Diamond: Sometimes, your players won't like it when you tell them to hustle in the outfield or run out ground balls or try another batting stance. They're reticent because—perhaps like too many coaches—they're used to a certain way of doing things and have been doing something the same way since Little League. You have to encourage change and ask that players give something new a chance before deciding what's best for themselves. Those players who don't—or won't—adjust won't last. That's their choice. But you can at least say you tried to help them extend their careers.

In the Workplace: Asking workers to stay late won't make you popular among them, but if you make the same commitment you ask from them, they will feel less upset about needing to work overtime or come in on a weekend. Plus, if you offer good incentives—and not just that you're buying pizzas—then they might even volunteer for such service in the future.

Lesson #79: Coach With Fortitude
Ken Schreiber

*"Don't let other people dictate
the way your team should play!"*

When *Collegiate Baseball* names you the High School Coach of the Century, you must be someone pretty special—and Ken Schreiber fits that description. In his 38 years as head baseball coach at LaPorte High School in northwest Indiana, Coach Schreiber won more than 1,000 games, 25 conference titles, 28 sectional championships, 18 regional titles, and a record seven state championships—including his 1987 team being named the national champions. He was recognized as Indiana Coach of the Year nine times, Midwest Coach of the Year four times, and National Coach of the year three years.

In *The Baseball Coaching Bible*, Coach Schreiber suggested that coaches ask themselves three questions before developing a baseball program:
- What type of coach do I want to be and what kind of coach am I capable of being?
- How much time am I willing to put forth in developing a program?
- How much latitude will my school administration and community allow me in building up a program?

He then detailed some critical aspects to building and/or enhancing a program:
- *Three-stage program:*
  1. *The summer schedule:* "Although we emphasize winning, this part of the program is mostly for observation, instruction, and experimentation."
  2. *The winter program:* This time "gives us the opportunity to work on a lot of one-on-one, individual-position instructions" because the team has been forced inside to a smaller facility, pushing the team to break down the game into smaller parts.
  3. *The regular season:* "We emphasize team drills, fundamentals, and strategies. Two weeks before the season opener, we devote additional attention to the pitching staff."
- *Program first, individual second:* "The principle of program first and individual second is based on the premise that the individual, though important to the program, will move on in a short time. The program will remain for other individuals to benefit from."
- *Setting realistic goals:* "If the coach sets goals so high that they are unreachable, the players will have difficulty developing confidence in themselves and the program. On the other hand, if the coach sets goals that are too easily accomplished, the players and the program could be functioning under false pretenses."
- *Do it your way:* "Thousands of books have been written … on the topic of how to play baseball. The successful coach will decide what methods and theories best fit his personality and then incorporate them into his program."

- *Basic before cute:* "If coaches emphasize the cute stuff"—pickoffs, hidden-ball tricks, and gimmicks plays—"at the expense of the basics of the game, they should not be surprised at their lack of success."
- *Time to coach, time to not:* "Regardless of how much knowledge a coach has, of equal importance is his ability to transfer it to his players constructively. ... Overcoaching can be just as detrimental as not coaching enough."

Leadership Lessons

On the Diamond: No matter if you're part of a new program somewhere or have been coaching for years, keep one premise in mind: You can only teach one thing at a time if you want to have success. Building and strengthening a program means doing so with the future in mind, not just today. To that end, you'll have better success right way if you can focus on one aspect about the game at a time. You might have assistants who are working with players in groups or you might be leading a full-team scenario, but stick to one dynamic at a time. One way to do this is to plan out a day's practice and enforce that schedule.

In the Workplace: How often have you been to a meeting where so many topics are discussed that once the hour is up, no decisions have been made about how to resolve those issues? To help your team or your employer achieve success, schedule brief meetings to discuss one topic at a time and how to handle it. Or forgo meetings entirely and conduct fact-finding missions via email. Just remember that workers will accomplish more if they're focused on one problem at a time. It's important to know who does what well because you can have several people working on several different issues simultaneously and not bother people who can't help with a particular problem.

Lesson #80: Define Your Potential—and Then Achieve It

Mike Scioscia

"Success is really just achieving your potential as a person. Whatever that potential is—to have it materialize and become achievement, I think, is success."

Because Mike Scioscia spent his all-star career catching Fernando Valenzuela and Orel Hershiser with the Los Angeles Dodgers, he learned how to manage games, pitchers, and other players. He brought a National League attitude to an American League team—and he has kept the Los Angeles Angels of Anaheim competitive in his 13 seasons through good pitching, strong defense, and quick runners. All this helped him bring a World Series title to Anaheim in just his third season on the bench.

Scioscia knows it's no easy road to success, but tempering achievements with strong and well-meaning expectations can help people reach their goals.

"Some of the toughest things to watch along the way (and I know it happens in all walks of life) is to watch people with incredible potential that don't realize it enough to where it becomes achievement. That's one of the toughest things. I think if you do get to that level, I consider that success," Scioscia said. "We're not all gonna set world records, we're not all gonna be all-stars, we're not all gonna become first in our class at Harvard Law, you know. Not that that shouldn't be a goal of yours, but the more pragmatic approach is to say, 'This is what I have, let me get to the level that I can achieve.' And that when you look back and you're satisfied with the way things have gone. If you've maximized what your potential is, that's success."

One way to help people work toward their dreams and find success is to take ownership of putting together the pieces needed to reach those dreams. In baseball—and in other walks of life—trades and free agent signings often prevent any given squad from coming up through the ranks together and continuing to play at the major league level. But when the opportunity exists to develop and retain, make the best of it—quickly.

"If you're not developing your own guys, scouting, drafting, and developing your own players, a philosophy we know is important, it's very, very tough to keep continuity and keep the team where it needs to be," Scioscia said. "This whole clubhouse really has a feel of player development in it, which is really the ultimate."

Leadership Lessons

On the Diamond: How do you help your players determine their potential as individuals and as a team? Why not ask them about their goals. Never tell someone his dream isn't worthwhile. In fact, you might be just the person to help him achieve it. But you'll never know by guessing or merely by watching someone. You're a leader—act like one by being an advocate for your players.

In the Workplace: Strive toward encouraging your employees to reach their potential, but ensure they have defined it first—as individuals and as part of a team. When people know their team goals and what they can offer to the greatest good, they're more apt to increase and enhance their personal goals and then gain confidence in them when they see their potential—their piece of the puzzle—is critical to team success. Just make sure you give your employees chances to reach their potential.

Lesson #81: Keep Positive Company
John Scolinos

*"We must remember we are preparing ballplayers
for successful everyday living, not merely
the next level of baseball."*

After serving as Pepperdine College's head baseball coach from 1946 to 1960, John Scolinos led California State Polytechnic University–Pomona from 1962 to 1991. Pomona won Division II College World Series titles in 1976, 1980, and 1983 as well as six California College Athletic Association championships, and Coach Scolinos earned Division II Coach of the Year honors three times.

In *The Baseball Coaching Bible*, Coach Scolinos noted eight life lessons that reflect baseball scenarios:
- Handling failure
- Handling fear
- Handling frustration
- Handling embarrassment
- Handling loneliness
- Handling slumps
- Adjusting to change
- Controlling emotions

He also wrote two great acrostics for trust and failure:
T: Thankful
R: Reliable
U: Understanding
S: Sincere
T: Truthful

F: Frustration
A: Aggressiveness
I: Insecurity
L: Loneliness
U: Uncertainty
L: Resentment
E: Emptiness

"Surround yourself with good people," Coach Scolinos said. "If you surround yourself with donkeys, they'll lead you to Donkeyville."

Leadership Lessons

On the Diamond: Once players are done in baseball, how will they do in the real world? Connect fundamentals to life lessons as often as you can. Ensure that each player feels like he has a comrade he can trust to help him when failure creeps in—and if that leader is you, all the better. Be the kind of leader you'd want someone to be for you. Have faith in yourself that you're helping to educate and lead the next generation of educators and leaders, not merely the next crop of great baseball players.

In the Workplace: You don't have to be a poet to eloquently offer life lessons to your employees. Not everything they do is life and death, but some tasks can equate to life experiences and how to handle them. Make an effort to show and explain those parallels in whatever ways feel comfortable to you. You can help your employees find success in business that will also help them in life.

Lesson #82: Tap Into Your Power Supply
Frank Selee

*"To make a success, a baseball manager must enter
into his work with every bit of energy he can command."*

Frank Selee is a too-often-forgotten manager who turned rowdy teams into winning teams with strong fundamentals: fielding bunts, employing hit-and-run situations, and stealing bases. Selee's greatest ability during his 13 seasons with the Boston Beaneaters (now the Atlanta Braves) and four seasons with the Chicago Orphans/Cubs was probably talent assessment. He could easily determine what a man could do and where he could best do it.

"He was a good judge of players," said former second baseman and Cubs captain Bobby Lowe. "He didn't bother with a lot of signals, but let his player figure out their own plays. He didn't blame them if they took a chance that failed. He believed in place-hitting, sacrifice-hitting, and stealing bases. He was wonderful with young players."

In Boston, this evaluation ability led to five National League pennants, including a 1898 team that featured Jimmy Collins, who would become the manager for the Boston Americans (now the Red Sox), which would win the first World Series in 1903. Collins started his career in the outfield but showed an adeptness at fielding bunts, so Selee moved him to third base, which gave Collins more playing time and boosted his offensive numbers.

In Chicago, Selee's keen eye for talent helped him put together the greatest double play trio ever: Tinker to Evers to Chance. Initially, shortstop Joe Tinker had been a third baseman, second baseman Johnny Evers had been a shortstop, and first baseman Frank Chance had been a catcher. When Selee became too ill to continue to manage in 1905, Chance took over and led the team to four National League pennants and two World Series titles in his first five full seasons. In fact, Tinker and Evers would also have their chance (no pun intended) to manage the Cubs, but they wouldn't match Chance's success in the Windy City nor Selee's in Boston. But it was Selee who had put together those great Cubs teams even if he didn't live to enjoy their success.

"If I make things pleasant for the players, they reciprocate," Selee said. "I want them to be temperate and live properly. I do not believe that men who are engaged in such exhilarating exercise should be kept in strait jackets all the time, but I expect them to be in condition to play. I do not want a man who cannot appreciate such treatment."

Leadership Lessons

On the Diamond: After you've been around a group long enough, you'll know what they can tolerate, and you'll have gone through other methods described in this book to assess their skills. Everyone has bad days and times when they feel lethargic and bothered by one issue or another. But you owe it to your players to meet and certainly try to exceed their energy level. Become involved in their practices by playing a position and become involved in their games by coaching first or third base—a practice that needs a revival at all levels. Players love being on the field. Shouldn't you enjoy that experience, too?

In the Workplace: Motivational speeches can become obnoxious and tiresome for some employees, but workers should enjoy a timely and energetic meeting to rally everyone around a goal or deadline. You can build bonds by being there for your employees—even when they need to stay late—and pitching in to help in whatever ways you can. When you can lessen burdens, you can earn respect, and when you earn such esteem, you'll have employees who enjoy working for you.

Lesson #83: Act Like Professionals
Dick Siebert

"We're going to show those fellows
that we're major leaguers."

Dick Siebert spoke those words after a game in 1960 against the University of Southern California—a perennial power at the time—about how he wanted his players to carry themselves on and off the field, including on the bus ride back to the hotel after that game. With that philosophy, "The Chief" helped change the tradition of baseball in the state of Minnesota in the late 1950s and early 1960s.

"After playing 17 years of professional baseball I thought I knew all there was to know about the game. I felt that my background alone entitled me to coach on a college level. Well, I was wrong. I discovered that all I really knew was how to play first base and how to hit. Other teams were beating us on pitching and fundamentals, and there were plenty of times when I was out-coached," Coach Siebert said about his early years at the University of Minnesota, where he coached from 1948 to 1978 and won three national titles (1956, 1960, and 1964).

Coach Siebert then started to study his opponents as well as read books about coaching. Like Connie Mack did as manager of the Philadelphia Athletics, he began to keep his own scorecard, allowing him to immediately know what a player had done offensively or defensively and then adjust his game strategy accordingly.

In his biography for the Baseball Biography Project for the Society for American Baseball Research, Rich Arpi noted Siebert's impact on baseball in the Gopher State: "The strength of the game of baseball in Minnesota today, from the little leagues to the high schools to American Legion programs and to colleges, is attributable to Dick Siebert's preaching his 'gospel of baseball' in countless clinics and seminars."

Those clinics and seminars included Coach Siebert coaching amateur teams during the off-season, allowing him to gauge local talent as well as coach his own players—a practice now forbidden by the NCAA but something that certainly helped Coach Siebert build some great Gopher teams during his tenure.

Leadership Lessons

On the Diamond: You don't have to have Major League–caliber players to have Major League attitudes. You also don't need to know all there is to know in order to manage. Take it upon yourself to do your own homework and gain skills in your weaker areas—but don't forget to continue developing your strengths. Likewise, consider keeping a scorecard during games to not only keep you involved in the game, but to also help you see where you can make changes. Such a scorecard should include batting, pitching, and defensive plays.

In the Workplace: Most managers earn their positions through what they've learned in roles now filled by their employees. But you can always find areas to improve in, and you should take time to gain extra training—whether onsite or perhaps through online means—to enhance your managing skills as well as strengthen your weaknesses. Remember, your employees look to you for guidance, so it makes sense to ensure you have the knowledge to help them.

Lesson #84: Respond to Situations
Hal Smeltzly

*"The ability to focus on the task at hand is what
separates successful players and teams from the losers."*

In 20 years as a head baseball coach—most notably at Florida Southern College—Hal Smeltzly won almost 400 games and won three Division II national titles (in 1971, 1972, and 1975). He earned National Coach of the Year honors in 1972, and he also coached teams on the international level, including the Netherlands' national team in 1967 and 1971.

In *The Baseball Coaching Bible*, Coach Smeltzly wrote about leadership style:

> To be a successful coach, you must work at keeping your people skills appropriate and effective. Review your thought processes. What assumptions or convictions about certain things, ideas, or individuals do you hold as true? For example, coaches have preconceived attitudes about human nature and what makes players respond. Some coaches believe that reward and discipline should be used only in exceptional cases. Most of the time they will choose to go with the flow when working with players. This leadership style works better with older, more experienced players. ...

> You must make a decision about what leadership style best suits you and your team. Selecting the correct style of leadership requires you to evaluate the situation. Consider how skillful, motivated, and committed your players are to having a successful season. These are critical factors as they will definitely influence your efforts to communicate. Your players must understand your intent, so that they will want to help you and the team accomplish a successful season. Inexperienced players will need your direction. You will have to tell them what they should do and how they should do it. For a team with returning players, you will need to assess the level of direction required. As the team gains some competence and experience, the players will become even more motivated. As players develop, you will find that you can gradually take a more flexible style. This can apply to the individuals or to the team as a whole. Times will come, however, when you may need to return temporarily to the direct style of leadership.

Leadership Lessons

On the Diamond: When your team loses a big lead, how do you react? When do you react? When do you let go? How do you handle the aftermath? You don't have to change how you coach as much as you need to reaffirm the way you coach. Being resolute will help you portray the best image possible to your players and gain the best effort from them.

In the Workplace: When a minor or major catastrophe hits, how do you handle it? Do you have a process in place for every problem? Maybe not. And maybe that's a good thing because spontaneous situations encourage you to think on your feet. You don't have to change your management style as much as you need to acknowledge what works best for you—and know that your employees admire it, too.

Lesson #85: Expand Your Vision
Bob Smith

*"From the beginning of any relationship,
take the big picture approach."*

Bob Smith coached collegiate baseball at Taylor University (Indiana) and Greenville College (Illinois) from 1958 to 1976 before becoming president of the U.S. Baseball Federation and supporting the idea of making baseball an Olympic sport again (which it had been off and on from 1904 to 1964). He succeeded in this endeavor, as baseball was a consistent Olympic sport from 1984 to 2008.

In *The Baseball Coaching Bible*, Coach Smith offered counterattacks to temptations to not be a coach with integrity:

- *Lead by example:* "Finding the proper balance"—with work, home, and faith—"makes life much more rewarding and it enables you as a coach to be the role model who consistently walks his talk."
- *Play by the rules:* Keep them in mind and ensure your players know them too.
- *Practice honest salesmanship regarding your program:* "Integrity begins at the mouth. Your word must be trustworthy. … Do not promise a player or his parents some lofty hope that goes beyond what you can deliver."
- *Win with sportsmanship:* Intimidation not only makes you look bad but also hurts your reputation and credibility.
- *Look out for your players' health:* "Install a team trainer or doctor with unquestionable veto power over you and leave medically related judgments to the doc."
- *Support your institution or organization:* Players need to know an organization's mission and strive to showcase it in all ways—not just on the baseball field.
- *Be humble in victory; gracious in defeat:* "There are certainly lessons to be learned from losing. One of the most important is how to lose with a sense of respect for your opponent and a willingness to accept and learn from your mistakes and defeat."

Leadership Lessons

On the Diamond: Morals and ethics go hand in hand. Ensure your players know what's right, what's wrong, and what the rulebook says. Cheaters seldom prosper. Too many programs have had sanctions placed on them in recent years. Stay focused on the big picture—how will decisions today impact players well after they've left a program?

In the Workplace: Employee handbooks are but one way to ensure employees are being moral and ethical. Being a whistleblower isn't an ideal situation for anyone, but in your managerial role, you must prevent and eliminate suspicious activity and ensure to report it. Your company's image is more important than a little graft and a major scandal.

Lesson #86: Compete With the Best

Tracy Smith

*"There is a big difference between
the most talented and the 'best.'"*

Tracy Smith took over a successful Indiana Hoosiers program in 2006 and has heightened its prominence in recent years, including leading Indiana University to its first Big Ten tournament title since 1996 and just its second NCAA tournament appearance. He has also had at least one freshman each season from 2008 to 2011 earn All-American honors. In recent years, Coach Smith has focused more on recruiting and making Indiana more than just a basketball state. He has developed some pointed thoughts about coaching collegiate baseball:

- *On recognition:* "I have always believed coaches give themselves too much credit when it comes to players performing well. At IU, we try to instill an attitude of ownership in our kids. If you do well, take the credit. If you do poorly, don't start pointing fingers."

- *On coaching:* "I love the daily interaction with my team. I love meeting new people through my job. Baseball, particularly being the coach at IU, allows me to be in some pretty unique settings."

- *On competition:* "I think sometimes kids are afraid to compete. They want things handed to them. There is nothing better than competition and adversity to help players grow."

- *On development:* "Outwork the guy next to you and don't be afraid of failure. This game is built around failure. There are no shortcuts to success!"

Leadership Lessons

On the Diamond: Encouraging competition is easier than it seems—but has to be done with tact and without belittling someone. One way to do this is through open tryouts every year. While you might know that a player is a lock to be your third baseman, don't let him know that. You'll have new players each year who might want to play third base, and to find out how dedicated someone is to earn that spot, you have to judge him in a new light by allowing others to field chances at that position. You'll learn really quickly if the player you think is a lock has an attitude for a locked player.

In the Workplace: If you want to be a great manager, you have to allow your own actions, not those of your employees, to determine your self-worth. You can't live vicariously through your employees nor take credit for their successes unless you're in the trenches with them. You're not competing with your employees. You're guiding them to a better place—as people and as employees. Take credit for what *you* do to better things.

Lesson #87: Swing for Compassion
Billy Southworth

"Gentlemen, swinging the bat is a great exercise. It strengthens the diaphragm and loosens pent-up emotions in the chest. Besides, you may hit the ball."

Billy Southworth had few easy roads during his 76 years—his wife died at age 42, his son died in a plane crash during World War II, and alcoholism nearly ruined his own life—but for a brief period in the 1940s, he and the St. Louis Cardinals were on top of the baseball world.

From 1942 to 1944, the Cards won the National League pennant and won the World Series twice—losing to the New York Yankees in 1943 despite not having Joe DiMaggio, who was serving his military duty. Those three teams also won more than 100 games each season—a feat not accomplished in franchise history before or since.

In 1948, when Southworth managed the Boston Braves (now in Atlanta) to its first National League pennant since 1941 and to the World Series against the Cleveland Indians (who would best his Braves in six games), he reflected on the kind of attitude he took as a manager.

"You don't have to have a good memory to recall the rebuffs you get as a youngster because even Time doesn't eradicate those scars," he said. "I guess I was a little thicker-skinned than most boys of my age, otherwise I couldn't have taken it as I did. Anyway, I promised myself that if I ever became a manager, I would treat a boy better than I was treated. I think I have kept the faith in that respect. Perhaps I've been forced to release a boy because he didn't have the ability to make my club, but there's none can say that I didn't treat him with kindness and respect."

"He just had a gut feeling about the right thing to do in a situation. The moves he would make would work for him—all the time, not occasionally," said former outfielder Clint Conatser, who played under Southworth with the Braves. "Leo Durocher was the same way. It's like some guys can pick horses out of nowhere. Southworth was a genius like that on the diamond."

Leadership Lessons

On the Diamond: Sometimes, you learn to do the opposite of what mentors show you in their actions and what they say in their words. You pick out the good aspects—or what you see as positive—and carry those through to your own leadership roles. But maybe you had a saintly coach and perhaps he countered your own rough attitude by being gentle with you—an opposite tactic as suggested here. You're driven by your personality, but when dealing with 25 other personalities, you can adjust your style much easier than 25 guys can change theirs.

In the Workplace: No matter if you supervise five employees or 100 employees, you're going to make an impact on someone with how you treat each person—and what others see when they observe those interactions. As much as you'd like to treat everyone the same and apply the same rules, being flexible will allow you to properly address problems as well as heap praise without creating an envious atmosphere for other employees.

Lesson #88: Put Pressure Aside

Jack Stallings

*"Discipline and poise in practice become discipline
and poise in the final moments of a game!"*

In his 39 years as a college baseball coach with Wake Forest University, Florida State University, and Georgia Southern University, Jack Stallings won 1,258 games and led Georgia Southern to five NCAA Regionals and one College World Series appearance.

In an article for BaseballTips.com, Coach Stallings discussed how to play well under pressure:

> The ability to play well under pressure is one of the most desired qualities for any athlete in any sport, and a player who can perform extremely well in practice but cannot duplicate that performance in a game will not be successful and will, in fact, be a very frustrated athlete.

> The first step in dealing with pressure is to recognize and accept the fact that pressure is being created. To deal effectively with pressure, we must acknowledge it exists and then learn how to handle it properly and effectively. Pressure is created not by the game situation but by how we look at it and how we handle it. It is not the situation or someone else making us tense, it is us! We create pressure by how we think or act, not by the situation we are in at the moment. ...

> Every game should be important and should be approached by the coach and every player on the team as if this game is the only one the team has a chance to win because it is the only one it is playing! To place any more importance on one game is to get out of the consistent preparation and consistent performance so vitally needed to be a consistent athlete who can perform properly under pressure. ...

> The objective under pressure should not be to play super because that is an unreasonable goal; the objective of an athlete should be to play normally under pressure. A former coach used to say, "When the game is on the line, all I want is for each player to just do his job." If each player will do his job normally in a pressure situation, the team will perform well and will be successful a good percentage of the time. Coming through under pressure is a percentage action. If a hitter is averaging .333 and gets a hit one time in three clutch situations, he is performing well in the clutch. Normal performance under pressure is the goal, not super performance.

Leadership Lessons

On the Diamond: Don't practice to defend or attack your opponent against something special you know it does, such as the first batter bunting or a pitcher who always throws from the stretch. Your players should play as normally as they always do and instead try to force the other team into mistakes with their tactics. It becomes a game of wits and psyche at that point—and a game of talents. You'll lessen pressure—and mistakes—when you allow players to play today's game just as they have every game before.

In the Workplace: When implementing new processes, you should try to retain how people go about their jobs and how they can incorporate new tasks into the work they already do. Most people disdain change, but it's inevitable. To make it smoother, allow workers to keep doing what they've always done in terms of their work, but reframe processes to fit nearly seamlessly into everyone's workflow. This approach might be more challenging in some situations, but unless you have to reinvent not just the wheel but every component of it, try to allow your employees to perform in their normal way and still weave in the new responsibilities.

Lesson #89: Reframe Your Criticism
Casey Stengel

"Managing is getting paid for home runs someone else hits."

Perhaps no manager had more high highs and low lows in his managerial career than Charles "Casey" Stengel. And during no period in American League history has a manager and a team so dominated baseball as did The Old Perfessor and the New York Yankees from 1949 to 1960. Only twice during that period—in 1954 by Al Lopez's Cleveland Indians, and in 1959 by Lopez's Chicago White Sox—did the Yankees not win the American League pennant.

Stengel and the Yankees did, though, win 10 pennants and seven World Series, including an unprecedented and an unmatched five straight from 1949 to 1953. "There is less wrong with this team than any team I have ever managed," Stengel said about those teams.

His managing experience before then—with the Brooklyn Dodgers (now in Los Angeles) and the Boston Bees/Braves (now in Atlanta)—and his managing experience after—with the expansion New York Mets as their first manager—pale in comparison to his time with the Yankees, but as his obituary in *Sports Illustrated* in 1975 noted, Stengel "couldn't have done it without his players":

> Oh, he could entertain friends—and anyone else within hearing distance—and leave them helpless with laughter, but he never played the fool for them, not even when he was lying on the floor of a hotel lobby at two in the morning, demonstrating the proper execution of the hook slide. He was lecturing, teaching, telling, explaining, illustrating, his arms waving, fingers gesturing, mouth grimacing, eyes winking. He was noted for saying, "You could look it up," but a more significant pet expression was, "Now let me ask you this." Like Socrates, he would pursue a theme with his listeners—his students—and the insights he would develop were sometimes astonishing.

> Contrary to what people thought who laughed at him without really listening to him, he almost always made sense. Not that he was easy to understand. His monologues wandered, his references were cryptic, his descriptions fragmentary. But he was a genius—quick, intuitive, loaded with bits and pieces of information that he would whip out and apply to a situation. If you knew his subject and the people he was talking about, what he said was a revelation. "My God," said a reporter hearing him for the first time, "he talks the way James Joyce writes."

"All blame is a waste of time. No matter how much fault you find with another, and regardless of how much you blame him, it will not change you," Stengel said. "The only thing blame does is to keep the focus off you when you are looking for external reasons to explain your unhappiness or frustration. You may succeed in making another feel guilty about something by blaming him, but you won't succeed in changing whatever it is about you that is making you unhappy."

Leadership Lessons

On the Diamond: Players love to know they're doing something well, but they also need to know when they're doing something wrong. You should always strive to let a player know something good about his efforts before giving his advice on something he's not doing well. How you criticize is a reflection of who you are, and if you want to see positive changes on your team, offering respect and firm yet careful feedback will earn you respect and dedication in return.

In the Workplace: Remember, if you didn't have workers, nothing would ever get done. When your workers know how you feel about them—the good and the bad—and they know you presented that assessment in helpful ways, they'll gladly make the needed changes to ensure work continues to go well and that everyone keeps striving toward reaching common goals.

Lesson #90: Make a Difference
Gene Stephenson

"The people that you leave behind, the people you have had some influence with, did you help them in some way become more successful? Did you give them some guidance along the way, even if it was some anecdote that helped them in some small way to have a better life? It's not rocket science. It's just about making a difference."

When Gene Stephenson became the head coach at Wichita State University in 1977, the Shockers didn't have a team or a field or equipment. In his almost 35 years running the baseball program at WSU, Coach Stephenson has led the team to almost 1,800 wins (second most in Division I baseball behind Augie Garrido), 20 regular season conference titles, and 15 Missouri Valley Conference tournaments. His 1989 Shockers team won the College World Series.

In a 2009 interview with the *Wichita Business Journal*, Coach Stephenson explained his five basic principles that help him lead his team:

- *Deserve:* Stephenson reminds his players to look at the press box at Eck Stadium to see accomplishments achieved by previous teams. This helps put deserved success in perspective.
- *Desire:* Playing against colleges with more fans and bigger budgets should provide a motivation to beat those teams.
- *Dream:* "Don't be afraid to dream big. Everybody can dream big dreams, but if they're not willing to work hard to achieve those … then they are going to fall by the wayside."
- *Discipline:* "We say to these guys, practice winning at everything that you're responsible for. If you're responsible for going to class and being a good student, practice being a winning student."
- *Dimension:* "This is keeping everything in proper perspective—never being too high, never being too low. Always recognize that today is a new day."

Leadership Lessons

On the Diamond: You don't have to have philosophies or pithy comments to encourage your players to win. You don't have to have a deep tradition at your school or on your team to show your players how winning works. Use your physical and vocal leaders as examples, and don't hesitate to start new traditions—even if you change them every year. If your program doesn't have a history of success, preach to your players that they have the chance to put their team on the baseball map and that future teams will talk about *them.*

In the Workplace: Most businesses and companies have some history and perhaps some traditions, but your employees don't need to feel immersed in that for you to explain how important their work is toward achieving goals on personal and professional levels. You can offer daily mantras and have weekly meetings to help motivate everyone, but workers will likely prefer to rely on their own prior successes for helping them through tough times. If you can connect your team's current need for success to past successes—depending on your history and/or knowledge of your place of employment—then you build bridges that help employees see how vital they are to the public's image and to the company's credibility.

Lesson #91: Seek Middle Grounds

Ray Tanner

*"We've gotten better, but as I reminded the team there is
just a few steps between the outhouse and the penthouse.
You've got to play with heightened awareness all the time."*

When Ray Tanner retired from coaching college baseball after the 2012 season, he certainly went out on top: His South Carolina Gamecocks won two straight College World Series in 2010 and 2011, and Coach Tanner won the National Coach of the Year award in both seasons. In fact, in 2012, Coach Tanner took his team to the title series again but lost both games to Andy Lopez and the University of Arizona Wildcats.

Coach Tanner preached confidence and consistency with his teams. Most players who play college baseball were stars on their high school teams, but it's harder for some players—especially underclassmen—to make their mark on a talented and successful team.

"Always keep a positive attitude and be ready for your opportunity," he said about such players. "Work hard and continue to improve even if you're not getting consistent playing time. You never know when your chance will come. I had a freshman outfielder who played well early in the year when he was filling in for our injured starting outfielder. He played well, but sat right back down on the bench and played sparingly the rest of the year. Late in the season when we were struggling on offense I threw him in the mix for a few games and he caught fire. He ended up hitting over .400 for the NCAA tournament and making the College World Series All-Tournament Team. He kept a positive attitude and stayed ready. That really impressed me."

Coach Tanner also knew that player success depended as much—if not more—on the player himself than anything he could provide from a coaching standpoint.

"If you want to get better, you have to invest. You have to put in the time that's necessary to make it to that next level," he said. "Is that a guarantee that you will get a good return on your investment? No, but the guarantee is that if you don't invest it's not going to happen. That's almost a definite. You can't just say, I want to do this or I want to accomplish that. You actually have to live it. You have to show it. And if you do invest, then just maybe it comes to pass, but if it doesn't work out, at least at the end of the day you can look yourself in the mirror and say, 'You know what—I did the best I could.'"

Leadership Lessons

On the Diamond: One way to prepare for role players is to ensure you're always involving them during practice. This might mean breaking players into groups that aren't weighed heavily with regulars or role players in any of them. You never know when a regular might learn something from a role player. And you never know when injuries or other issues might come up, and when role players are just as familiar with situational hitting or pitching as regular players, they'll perform well when their time does come.

In the Workplace: If you have an administrative assistant, or an intern, or others who might come and go throughout a project's lifetime who are as involved with the everyday tasks that go on—whether through meetings or doing hands-on work or even job shadowing—as those who are consistent and established workers, then those people can come in handy when workloads become too much or someone just needs a break. Never neglect those who are learning, and remember to offer opportunities to those who want to learn.

Lesson #92: Swing With Confidence
Bill Terry

"Hitting is business. With two strikes you really protect that plate."

Bill Terry had the unenviable task of taking over as manager for the New York Giants after John McGraw's 31-year reign in that position. In his first full season (1933), he led the team to its first National League pennant since 1924 (a long time in many Giants' fans' minds after enjoying 10 of them during McGraw's time) and then beat the Washington Senators to win the World Series. He did this while also playing first base for the team, which he would continue to do through the 1936 season, when the Giants won their second pennant under Terry—and would do so again in 1937, losing to the New York Yankees in the World Series both seasons.

"He was a good manager. He knew the game. When you play under a man like John McGraw all those years, you learn the game," said Leo Durocher, who played and managed against Terry.

Although the 1933 Giants had an amazing pitching staff—anchored by future Hall of Famer Carl Hubbell—the team's success, as it had been for most of the franchise's existence, had been hitting. Terry knew that confidence in one's abilities could serve any hitter well.

"I don't mean a fellow can start right out knocking a ball lopsided by simply saying to himself he can do it," Terry said. "What I do mean is that if you want to accomplish something, you must have confidence in your method of doing it."

Leadership Lessons

On the Diamond: Who was the coach who made a difference to you? Who encouraged you to become a coach? Remember, the players you coach might one day have the aptitude and desire to coach. You're serving as a role model to them. You do this through confidence and through taking responsibility, especially when you're in a tough situation and have but one strike left.

In the Workplace: In some workplaces, managers still come from within the working ranks. What manager inspired you? Who did you learn from? Keep these people in mind as you lead your workers because some of them might want your job when you move on or move up. Mentoring is as much a part of your job as managing.

Lesson #93: Trust Your Words
Joe Torre

"Communication is the key to trust, and trust is the key to teamwork in any endeavor, be it sports, business, or family."

When Joe Torre took over the New York Yankees in 1996, the team hadn't won a World Series since 1978—its longest drought in franchise history since winning its first title in 1921. He proceeded to lead the team to four World Series titles in five years—a feat bested only by former Yankee managers Joe McCarthy and Casey Stengel.

In his 1999 book *Joe Torre's Ground Rules for Winners*, Torre listed 12 keys to managing not only successes but also enduring and overcoming setbacks:

1. Knowing your team players
2. Fairness, respect, and trust
3. Straight communication
4. Maintaining serenity
5. Sustaining optimism
6. Trusting your intuition
7. Creating mutual respect and trust
8. Asserting your agenda—and your integrity
9. Deference, distance, and dialogue: striking the balance
10. Handling setbacks
11. Caring, conviction, and commitment
12. Sacrificing yourself

Perhaps no manager during George Steinbrenner's ownership tenure lobbied more and asserted himself more than Joe Torre. His opportunity to manage a great collection of baseball players came after disappointing stints with three teams in the National League. He showed the American League that a team could play National League–style baseball if it could adhere to his core principles. Plus, it doesn't hurt to have an extra batter in the lineup by being able to enjoy a designated hitter in the American League.

Or perhaps his success came from taking a new approach to managing. As he said: "I try to understand what motivates other people. Some players may be critical of a decision I make, but I'm more into 'Why did they say it?' as opposed to what they said."

Leadership Lessons

On the Diamond: At your first practice, you have to establish how players should communicate not just with you, but with other coaches and other players. You build trust by allowing fun and excitement to permeate throughout practices and games. When you start to hold players back from exhibiting their passion in their own way, they become too self-conscious and will overthink every decision they need to make throughout a practice or a game. Players tend to know themselves from their classes or from being on the same team for a long period of time, and because coaches and managers are often the first to go on any team, players build trust among themselves and desire a manager who eases himself into that camaraderie rather than one who too strongly asserts his power. Allow the team to dictate some of the ground rules, and you'll find that coaching them becomes much easier.

In the Workplace: How do you communicate with your workers? Through yelling? Through patient lessons? How can you tell which method works? Don't be fooled into thinking your workers are succeeding because you yelled at them in meetings and even in their work areas. Spend a week engaged in another communications method, and you might see your workers' attitudes change and their work ethic become even better than when you were yelling. If they don't, then an underlying reason exists for poor performance, but yelling won't solve that either.

Lesson #94: Educate Yourself

Glen Tuckett

*"Self-confidence is critical to
decision making and decisiveness."*

During Glen Tuckett's 17 years at Brigham Young University, he won 498 games and led the Cougars to two College World Series appearances. He later served as the athletic director at BYU and at the University of Alabama.

In *The Baseball Coaching Bible*, Coach Tuckett noted advice for coaches about personal and professional development:

- The greatest gift we can bestow upon others is a good example.
- A confused player cannot be aggressive. Prepare your players.
- Make a conscious effort to praise a player's positive performance in words rather than assuming he is aware of how you feel.
- Don't be reluctant to put your arm around his neck. Let him know you like him.
- Instruct. Don't punish. Express displeasure in a positive, impersonal manner.
- Few players have become poorer players because of compliments from a coach, but many players are driven to self-doubt by a coach's sarcastic criticism.
- Help the player develop a positive self-image built by repeated (sometimes small) successes.
- Shine up or polish your players' halos.
- Hold the mirror at the most flattering angle.
- Reenshrine the nobility of work. The work ethic can be taught. Baseball is a year-round game, a way of life, not just a spring pastime. Hard work is a foolproof confidence builder. Those who have worked the hardest are the last to surrender.

Leadership Lessons

On the Diamond: You might think all your players understand what to do in any given situation, but this is why you train and practice. You build up a young man's sense of worth when you acknowledge he has done something well and give him motivation to do better when he's made an error, but it's all about tone, diction, and reinforcement: Say it politely but firmly in easy-to-understand terms, and then reiterate that information by allowing the player to test himself again—and once he's attempted it a few times, then you can offer more feedback as needed. Don't interrupt a player while he's trying to work through a problem.

In the Workplace: Everyone likes to know he's doing something well, but when you need to let an employee know that he had made an error, you have two positive options: You can ask him to do it again—politely yet firmly and without accusations—or you can take the time to show the employee what needs to be done. You don't have to use the same method every time—your awareness of each employee will help you decide which will work best with whom—but these are great ways to be positive and helpful to your employees without degrading them.

Lesson #95: Seek Greatness
Gary Ward

"If you wish to be great, study those who are great."

In his 21 seasons as a college baseball coach, Gary Ward won 1,022 games and took the Oklahoma State Cowboys to 10 College World Series, including seven straight from 1981 to 1987. OSU also won 16 consecutive Big Eight titles, earning Coach Ward four Conference Coach of the Year awards.

In *The Baseball Coaching Bible*, Coach Ward offered his "seven lucky ideas" for coaches to include in their long-term goals:

- No great deeds can be achieved without the investment of passion into a goal that borders on obsession. Great hitters have an undying passion for hitting.
- There is magic in the power of belief. What you believe to be true becomes true when you believe it is possible. Great hitters believe they can hit.
- Create a strategic personal plan that organizes all your resources and those of your teaching laboratory. Great hitters have a strategy.
- Clarify your values. Make clear and specific judgments about what is important to you. Great hitters establish clearly defined, specifically written goals.
- Express an energetic joy for teaching. Bring enthusiasm to the learning environment. Anticipate discovery with each teaching session. Great hitters expend the energy.
- Invest yourself in your players. Develop the ability to bond with players and parents. Great hitters invest themselves in and trust their coaches.
- Prepare to become a master communicator. Your ability to communicate with others will determine the quality of your life and the quality of your leadership. Great hitting coaches are great communicators.

Leadership Lessons

On the Diamond: When you were a kid, who did you think was great? Who were your heroes? Who got you interested in baseball? Share those stories with your players. Encourage them to find someone to admire—in life and in baseball. And remind them to pay attention to how they carry themselves because others might consider them great and wish to admire them.

In the Workplace: How did you decide to go into the field you're in? Who inspired you when you were young? Who was your idol growing up? Share those people with your employees. And let them share their heroes with you. Focus on becoming great as individuals and as a team.

Lesson #96: Adjust to Adversity
Ron Washington

"Whenever one of those styles is needed, I know how to use it. If I have to take it to the opposing team, I will. If the team is going well, I'll kick back and watch them play. If my offense is struggling, then I have to do something to help get them over it. You adjust to whatever the situation is."

No team in Texas Rangers history has put on such offensive, defensive, and pitching displays as have the 2010–2012 teams. Not since the 1998 and 1999 teams had the Rangers made the playoffs two straight years—let alone three. But this recent Rangers team did the earlier team one better by going to two consecutive World Series. Although they lost both (to the Giants in 2010 and the Cardinals in 2011), the Rangers proved to baseball that a tide had turned in Arlington.

One main reason for this new atmosphere is manager Ron Washington. He doesn't allow his emotions to overtake him when dealing with mistakes or when arguing a call. His young team has taken notice, especially Josh Hamilton, who has rebounded from his many struggles in his career.

"He's a great player's manager. If he tells you something, you can believe it. If you need to go see him, you can. Otherwise he lets you go play and gave fun ... as long as it's the right way. If it's not, he'll let you know," Hamilton said.

Washington has made the best of his first Major League managing experience, and he credits that to being a quick learner. It also helped that the Rangers organization developed or brought in the needed players to compete for pennants and World Series titles. While Washington knows what needs to be done in any given situation, he also encourages his players to take advantage of situations if they know it will benefit the team and isn't taking too much of a risk. But above all, his easygoing communication style is effective and embraced by the team.

"As the years come and go, you get more comfortable with what you're doing and you begin to trust your instincts," Washington said. "You trust your players and coaches. You trust what you're doing. Without that trust, we wouldn't find ourselves where we are now."

And that place is as a dominant force in the American League.

Leadership Lessons

On the Diamond: Don't forget to build trust with your players. They must learn to make in-game decisions on their own if they're going to enjoy continued success. Micromanaging prevents players from really learning the game as well as learning from their mistakes. During a segment of practice—whether you do this once a day or a couple times a week—allow one player to "manage" the team to see what unfolds. Use that as a teaching moment.

In the Workplace: When times are tough, how do you adjust to it? Do you talk *with* (rather than *to*) your workers? When possible, give each worker a chance to lead a project and guide as needed but use the experience as a way to inform and educate rather than berate and force a my-way-or-the-highway attitude.

Lesson #97: Perform With Poise

Earl Weaver

"Good ballplayers make good managers, not the other way around. All I can do is help them be as good as they are."

Earl Weaver has been called a managerial genius. He tended to go with the percentages, he preferred three-run home runs to stolen bases, and he never hesitated to argue a call. Indeed, his 94 ejections during his 18-year career remain an American League record. But with teams flush with talent in those 18 seasons (including six Hall of Famers), no wonder many consider him one of the greatest managers ever—even if that moniker didn't always fit during the postseason.

Weaver's bombastic managing style helped his team to six first-place finishes and seven second-place finishes, including five seasons with more than 100 wins. His four pennants, including three straight from 1969 to 1971, proved that even a tough manager can encourage a team to produce its best. And although he won just one World Series—beating Cincinatti's newly minted Big Red Machine in 1970—his regular season achievements still stand as perhaps the best showing by an American League team in the 1970s.

Weaver understood how the right approach could help a team turn itself around. "Earl was so serious about winning," Hall of Fame third baseman Brooks Robinson said. "He used reverse psychology. When we were playing great, that was when he was on our backs—and when we weren't winning, that's when he was patting us on the back and telling us how great we were."

Of course, with Brooks Robinson manning the hot corner, Frank Robinson pounding home runs, and Jim Palmer mowing down batters—along with other players, such as Boog Powell (who won the American League MVP in 1970), Mike Cuellar, Dave McNally, and future manager Davey Johnson, performing beyond expectations—Weaver easily earned his place among baseball's greatest managers.

"People often talk about how many games a manager can win, but what wins games is how the players perform. When the manager makes out a lineup card, chooses a pinch-hitter or makes a pitching change, he's playing a part in the game," Weaver said. "Knowing when to get a guy out of the lineup is probably one of the most important, and toughest, parts of managing. If a guy goes hitless in four or five games and you take him out, did you make a mistake only the last time you played him, or every time? Did you make a mistake because he might be ready to break loose? Getting a guy out of the lineup at the right time is important, but it's just as important to have him in at the right time."

Leadership Lessons

On the Diamond: When your team wins, who takes credit? Remember, the manager can't win games or lose them on his own. But making the right choices in the right situations isn't easy. It takes practice—just like the practice your players need to perform well and win games for their manager.

In the Workplace: Acknowledging your workers with small tokens and public admiration will go a long way toward building confidence and, hopefully, encouraging others to want to earn that respect and those accolades—for the good of the team, not just for the manager's approval.

Lesson #98: Prepare to Prepare
Dick Williams

"Coaches don't win games.
They prepare players to win games."

In 1966, the Boston Red Sox finished ninth in the American League and had not had a third-place or better finish since 1958, let alone a World Series appearance since 1946. They hired Dick Williams to manage, and the team enjoyed a 20-game turnaround and won the 1967 American League pennant by a narrow one game over the Detroit Tigers and Minnesota Twins. Although the Red Sox would lose the World Series to the St. Louis Cardinals, Williams had clearly brought a new style to Boston.

Although the team couldn't sustain that magic, Williams did reproduce it when he went to Oakland in 1971, where he led the Athletics to three straight first-place finishes and two straight World Series titles in 1972 and 1973. Williams left the A's after the 1973 season after a disagreement with management about an injured Mike Andrews and went on to manage mediocre California Angels and Montreal Expos teams before taking over in San Diego in 1982, although the Expos did make their first and only playoff appearance in 1981 after Williams had been fired late in the strike-shortened season.

But no matter where he managed, Williams wasn't afraid to speak his mind.

"It's the most overused word in baseball. When my teams have gone well, it has been said I'm a good communicator. When they have gone bad, it has been said I've lost the ability to communicate," he said. "But the truth is, through all of it, I have been my same obnoxious self. People confuse communication with execution. Once a team has been taught to play, it starts losing only because it stops executing."

Although baseball hasn't changed much in its history, its players certainly have—and the reasons differ from person to person, making it difficult to apply a simple bandage.

"Today's manager must be a psychiatrist as well as baseball strategist. Many games have been won by figuring out what a player is thinking and how a pat on the back is much better than a kick in the rear," Williams said. "Maybe the old-time managers could give an inflexible order, but today's players don't roll over that easily. A manager must think of his player as an individual with completely different problems from any other player."

Leadership Lessons

On the Diamond: You're not just preparing people to win baseball games—you're preparing people to handle situations in everyday life. If you're working with young men, you can turn any activity into a chance to educate them on a life lesson. For example, having them hustle to first base on an infield ground ball could turn into a discussion about how they shouldn't give up on something because you never know what might happen: a player might bobble the ball, you might have success the next time you try, or something unexpected might happen and change everything.

In the Workplace: You'll never know what's going on in your workers' personal lives unless you ask—and do so in a way where you come across as compassionate and willing to help rather than as someone who's trying to hinder someone from resolving issues or pretending care to enhance your own image. Limits to communication do exist, but it's better to try to talk with your employees than to pretend everything is fine.

Lesson #99: Require Goals—and Require Success
John Winkin

*"Identify your goal for the day and
what you must do to accomplish it."*

John Winkin spent his 42-year college coaching career (from 1954 to 1996) in Maine—at Colby College and then at the University of Maine—and won 943 games, and he took 12 teams to the NCAA Regional tournaments and six teams to the College World Series. He also won the College Division Coach of the Year award in 1965.

In *The Baseball Coaching Bible*, Coach Winkin discussed how to handle practicing indoors, which could occur for various reasons, such as weather, not-ready-for-play field conditions, or other factors. A good coach needs to ensure he keeps restrictions in mind when planning indoor practices.

What generally complicates planning indoor practice is a mandated time limit. It might be 90 minutes, 120 minutes, even 360 minutes, yet baseball practice is always scheduled in a facility that also schedules many other activities, such as softball, basketball, lacrosse, track, spring football conditioning, intramurals, whatever. Therefore, a coach always must prioritize. Practice goals need to be planned, organized, and implemented to get the most from each practice session.

Besides time constraints, coaches conducting indoor practices also must deal with space limitations in meeting the goals planned for each practice. I always depend on (1) establishing priorities for getting a team ready, (2) being well organized for each practice session, and (3) using the available space effectively for each planned practice.

I have always worried about two matters in preparing for preseason and planning indoor practices. First, can I give a fair tryout indoors to players wishing to try out for the squad? I long ago concluded that I cannot do that. I feel that at the college level tryouts are best accomplished in fall baseball. In high school, where many of the key players are multisport athletes, one has to count on summer baseball (summer amateur leagues, clinics, and so forth) to accomplish the "tryout."

Second, I never have adequate time in indoor practices to accomplish all the needed teaching experiences. Again, I work hard at planning and working to accomplish needed teaching experiences at the college level in fall baseball. For the high school level, I have had greater success teaching needed baseball skills in summer clinics and camps and other planned summer baseball experiences.

My basic premise in preseason has been (1) to know which players I needed to focus on to get ready for the season ahead and (2) to focus on correcting each player in each practice experience.

Leadership Lessons

On the Diamond: When you focus on one goal each day and recognize the limitations it might present in terms of achieving that goal, you can determine the best plan for reaching it. And you might find that you can only accomplish part of a goal today and might have to finish it tomorrow. If that's the case, don't have a goal for tomorrow—but at the same time, reassess your goal to ensure it's not too broad and thus requiring that second (or even third) day to try to achieve it. Never let space or time or even weather dictate what you can and can't achieve.

In the Workplace: Daily goals are commonplace in most work environments. But you can break those down even further to allow your staff to have something to constantly build on and gain confidence in as they work toward harder and more long-term goals. When you have a good idea of who on your staff can do what, you can ensure you don't allow time or talents or other uncontrollable dynamics to restrict or prevent your employees from meeting their goals.

Lesson #100: Demand Accountability
Bobby Winkles

"My number one rule was 'be on time.' If the players were not 10 minutes early, then they were late."

In his 13 seasons as the head coach at Arizona State University, Bobby Winkles won 524 games, five conference titles, and three College World Series in 1965, 1967, and 1969—the latter two won after seasons in which the team didn't appear in the College World Series.

Before he took over the ASU program in 1959—at age 29 and a year removed from playing Minor League Baseball mostly in the Chicago White Sox farm system—Coach Winkles wrote down some critical plans for how he would go about coaching college baseball:

- We will play hard for the entire game.
- No player will be bigger than the team, no matter how good he may be.
- We will play fast games.
- We will be a team with character.
- I will be friends with all high school coaches and major league scouts.
- Any high school player can try out for the freshman team.
- We will be a disciplined team. Discipline will be the same for all players, and it will be fairly applied.
- We will be in great physical shape.

Coach Winkles also drew up a list of rules: "They encompassed much more than behavior on the baseball field and during the game. They covered being a student, being a good citizen, keeping in touch with parents, developing character, adhering to a dress code and hair-grooming code, being responsible, being polite, and developing self-discipline."

Leadership Lessons

On the Diamond: Don't forget to hold yourself accountable. You're not perfect, and you'll gain more respect from your players when they see you "punish" yourself for mistakes. Maybe you run the bases with the players or you stand in the box against the team's best pitcher and show how to avert balls thrown at your body.

In the Workplace: While you probably have a boss who has his own set of requirements for you, you can't go wrong by demanding good leadership modeling from yourself. Your workers need to know you take your role seriously and that you're willing to suffer the same consequences as them when something goes wrong.

Lesson #101: Become Baseball
Harry Wright

"[You] must learn to be a sure catch, a good thrower—strong and accurate—a reliable batter, and a good runner, all to be brought out—if in you—by steady and persevering practice."

Before Wilbur and Orville succeeded in helping airplanes reach lofty heights, baseball had its own Wright brothers: George and Harry. Both grew up with a cricket player for a father, and when baseball started to gain more popularity after the Civil War, the duo eventually found themselves in Cincinnati, helping to put together baseball's first professional team: the Red Stockings. Experts and fans might point to Alexander Cartwright (who helped established rules) or Abner Doubleday (who never made such a claim) as the man who invented baseball, but Harry Wright was the one who turned baseball into a professional sport.

In an article in *The Sporting Life*, a writer acknowledged Wright's role: "Every magnate in the country is indebted to this man for the establishment of baseball as a business, and every patron for furnishing him with a systematic recreation. Every player is indebted to him for inaugurating an occupation by which he gains a livelihood, and the country at large for adding one more industry to furnish employment."

The Red Stockings won all 57 of its games in 1869 against National Association of Base Ball Players teams, but once the team lost a game in 1870, fans lost interest. Wright took his team to Boston—the franchise eventually became the Boston Braves before moving to Milwaukee and Atlanta, where it remains today—in 1871 and managed the team when it became part of the National League in 1876. His Boston teams won six pennants, and he would later manage in Providence and Philadelphia.

When the Boston Americans—a team in the fledgling American League (started in 1901)—changed its name in 1908 to the Red Sox, it did so in homage to Wright's teams.

An article in the *Cincinnati Enquirer* in the 1860s said this about Wright: "[Harry Wright] eats base-ball, breaths base-ball, thinks base-ball, thinks base-ball, dreams base-ball, and incorporates base-ball in his prayers."

Leadership Lessons

On the Diamond: Although practices can't solely focus on one aspect to the game or even delve into one life lesson at a time, they can help players more if they feel similar to a real game. Perhaps every other week, invite students and parents to donate nonperishable goods for entrance into an intrasquad game. Ask a couple vendors to sell their wares and not hold back on their enthusiasm. Have kids from young levels come with signs and noisemakers. Then, reinforce that while your players play baseball, people are going hungry, those vendors' families depend on their earning a paycheck, and that those youngsters are the future of this world.

In the Workplace: Never underestimate how effective a brief training session can be for your employees. If money to send people out for training isn't available and it's also not affordable to bring someone in, perhaps you can work with a training company to share knowledge with each other. This way, you're gaining what you need and also offering your knowledge to someone else. Training companies can always benefit from some area of expertise you and your employees have.

About the Author

Christopher Stolle has worked as a book editor for most of his professional life, but has also worked in sports departments at three newspapers—*European Stars and Stripes*, the *Austin American-Statesman*, and the *Charlotte Sun*—as a copy editor, writer, and page designer. He also worked in sports departments at his high school and college newspapers, including being the sports editor for both. Along with fellow staff members at the *Charlotte Sun*, he was nominated for a Pulitzer Prize in the Breaking News category for coverage of Hurricane Charley in 2004.

Stolle continues to pursue writing as a personal endeavor. He has published dozens of poems, several essays, and a handful of sports, music, and poetry columns. He's also working on various novels, including one about Roy Hitt, a professional Minor League pitcher who played one season for the Cincinnati Reds in 1907.

To allow him to follow in his father's footsteps, Stolle earned a B.A. in journalism and education from Indiana University and a certificate in publishing and editing from Florida State University. He can't imagine being anything but an Indiana Hoosier, and he loves spending time with his niece, Isabella, and harassing his mother, Mary Anne, about her Purdue Boilermakers.